ENDORSEMENTS

I have known Alan for many years in his capacity as a Bible teacher within our church. He has always promoted the reading of Scripture and possesses a rare love for the Word of God. I am pleased that he has taken the time to write on the primacy of the Bible. In a day when the authority of the Bible is being challenged, I am pleased that Alan is giving a whole book to highlight God's big story. As always, Alan earths the theological into clear and practical application. It is my desire that many will read *The Wardrobe* and encounter the kingdom of heaven.

    Stuart Bell – Founder of the Ground Level Network of churches and Senior Pastor of Alive Church, Lincoln.

Alan's latest book, *The Wardrobe*, is a departure from his popular devotional works – but a wonderful and truly invigorating one for all who want to learn how to properly study the Scriptures and go deeper with God! Revealing the extensive amount of study that he has immersed himself in over the past decades, *The Wardrobe* covers academic ground by necessity, but remains wholly accessible to the introductory student or reader of the Bible. Dive in and begin to drink deeply from the wells that Alan has dug for the reader!

    Dr Johnny Markin – Worship pastor and consultant

Alan Hoare is an insightful and thought-provoking theologian whose writing seamlessly blends deep spiritual insights with practical wisdom for living. His books contain profound truths accessible through rich metaphors and down-to-earth examples. Alan's work invites readers to see the sacred in the ordinary and cultivate a contemplative presence in everyday life. Alan provides a pastoral voice and a broad perspective; his writing provides nourishment for the soul and guidance for the spiritual journey. With a unique synthesis of theology and personal experience, Alan is a wise guide for those seeking spiritual growth, deeper understanding of scripture and a more meaningful life.

Paul & Joy Blundell – Location Pastors, Alive Lincoln North

'We are what we eat,' it has been said. The damaging effects of snacking and eating selective diets have come under global scrutiny. Diet-related illnesses have become alarmingly prevalent. When it comes to our spiritual and biblical diet, the concern is not so much about the capacity to 'digest' but about desire – appetite! Alan Hoare writes his latest book, *The Wardrobe,* as a man consumed with a passion to devour the Word of God. It is his daily food: The air he breathes. It has nourished a life of faithful service over many decades. His writings are thoroughly researched and reflect authentically his life and ministry.

Rev Canon Chris Bowater OSL – Pastor, worship leader, songwriter, author.

THE WARDROBE

Encountering the Kingdom of Heaven through the Bible

Alan Hoare

Broad Place
publishing
broadplacepublishing.co.uk

First published in Great Britain in 2024

Broad Place Publishing

https://broadplacepublishing.co.uk

email: admin@broadplacepublishing.co.uk

Copyright © Alan Hoare 2024

The author has asserted his right under Section 77 of the Copyright, Designs and Patents Act, 1988, to be identified as the author of the work.

All rights reserved. No portion of the book may be reproduced or transmitted in any form or by any means, electronic or mechanical, including photocopying and recording, or by any information storage and retrieval system, without permission in writing from the publisher.

Except where otherwise noted, all Scripture quotations are from The ESV® Bible (The Holy Bible, English Standard Version®), © 2001 by Crossway, a publishing ministry of Good News Publishers. Used by permission. All rights reserved.

Also used: Good News Translation® (Today's English Version, Second Edition) © 1992 American Bible Society. All rights reserved.

The Message Copyright © 1993, 2002, 2018 by Eugene H. Peterson.

New American Standard Bible® (NASB), Copyright © 1960, 1971, 1977, 1995, 2020 by the Lockman Foundation. All rights reserved.

Holy Bible, New Living Translation, copyright © 1996, 2004, 2015 by Tyndall House Foundation. Used by permission of Tyndall House Publishers, Inc. Carol Stream, Illinois 60188. All rights reserved.

Every effort has been made to seek permission to use copyright material reproduced above fair usage in this book. The author and publisher apologise for those cases where permission might not have been sought, and if notified, will formally seek permission at the earliest opportunity.

Many thanks to The Banner of Truth Trust, Edinburgh, for permission to use the extensive quote in chapter 2.

The views and opinions expressed in this work are those of the author and do not necessarily reflect the views and opinions of the publisher.

A catalogue record for this book is available from the British Library.

Paperback ISBN: 978-1-915034-91-5

Hardback ISBN: 978-1-915034-92-2

*This book is dedicated to Mo,
my wife and dearest companion
for fifty years.*

Also by the Author

Journey through the scriptures in the spirit of lectio divina with Alan's daily devotionals. Find out more at:

https://www.exploringscripture.co.uk

Or listen to the *Exploring Scripture* Podcast, available on all popular podcast platforms.

Contents

Acknowledgements	ix
What others have said about the Bible	xi
Foreword	xv
Preface	xvii
Introduction	1
Chapter 1	5
Where Did the Bible Come From?	
Chapter 2	31
Can I Trust the Bible?	
Chapter 3	51
The Big Story in the Old Testament	
Chapter 4	83
The Dark Pause in the Big Story	
Chapter 5	97
The Big Story in the New Testament	
Chapter 6	125
The Approach to the Bible	
Chapter 7	147
Starting to Read the Bible	
Chapter 8	163
The Voice of God in the Bible	
Chapter 9	183
Getting It Inside Me	
Chapter 10	203
Constructing Solid Beliefs from the Bible	
Appendix of Recommended Books	239
Bibliography	241
About the Author	246

Acknowledgements

Firstly, I want to thank four men who knowingly, and unknowingly, fanned my flame of desire to enter into the world of the Bible. They have inspired and challenged me and left me longing for more. I want to honour Dr Charles W. Slemming (1903-1974), Professor Ralph Shallis (1912-1986), Denis Clark (died 1981), and Bob Mumford. Their depth in the Scriptures produced profound yearnings to know the Lord through His Spirit and His Word.

Secondly, I want to thank Mo, my wife, who has constantly believed in me and released me to read, study and write. She sometimes teases me, saying that at times she feels she is married to a Bible study! Your grammatical skills came into their own during the hours spend poring over the proof-copy, and I am so grateful for you.

Thirdly, I want to thank those dear friends of mine who have encouraged me to do what I do. They have added their endorsements to some of my books.

This particular book has been a long time in the making. I am so grateful to Dr Robert Deurden and Professor Carole Brooke for their constant support and their fine editing skills. I am also indebted to my publishers, Broad Place Publishing, especially Joy Velykorodnyy and Natasha Woodcraft, for their incisive editing and recommendations, and their persistent desire to make sure you, the reader, hear my voice in this book. To Kathleen Albans, Ruth Johnson and Anna Velykorodnyy, thank you for the long hours painstakingly proofreading and providing invaluable feedback. I have learned so much from you all.

Thank you to Paul and Nicky Walker for your generosity in getting this book off the ground! You have always been such an encouragement to me.

Finally, I want to thank Luke Jeffrey. He has always believed in this book, and I am so grateful for his constant belief in me over the years. Your words of encouragement over coffee and cake the day we met face to face were among the deepest I have ever received.

What Others Have Said About the Bible

'I am profitably engaged in reading the Bible. Take all of this Book that you can by reason and the balance by faith, and you will live and die a better man. It is the best Book which God has given to man.'
Abraham Lincoln[1]

'I have always said, and also will say, that the studious perusal of the sacred volume will make better citizens, better fathers, and better husbands.'
Thomas Jefferson[2]

'The Bible is a harp with a thousand strings. Play on one to the exclusion of its relationship to the others, and you will develop discord. Play on all of them, keeping them in their places in the divine scale, and you will hear heavenly music all the time.'
William P. White[3]

---

[1] Carolyn Tennyson-Arkels, *Under the Influence*, (WestBow Press, 2014), p.27
[2] *The British Controversialist and Literary Magazine*, (HardPress Publishing, 2019), p.348
[3] Ibid, p.139

'I began to read the Holy Scriptures on my knees, laying aside all other books, and praying over, if possible, every line and word. This proved meat indeed and drink indeed to my soul. I daily received fresh life, light, and power from above.'
George Whitfield[4]

'I have thought, I am a creature of a day, passing through life, as an arrow through the air. I am a spirit come from God, and returning to God: just hovering over the great gulf; till a few moments hence, I am no more seen. I drop into an unchangeable eternity! I want to know one thing, the way to heaven: how to land safe on that happy shore. God himself has condescended to teach the way; for this very end he came from heaven. He hath written it down in a book! Oh give me that book!'
John Wesley[5]

'One gem from that ocean is worth all the pebbles from earthly streams.'
Robert Murray McCheyne[6]

"The Christian Scriptures are the primary text for Christian spirituality. Christian spirituality is, in its entirety, rooted in and shaped by the scriptural text."[7]

---

[4] Arnold Dallimore, *George Whitfield,* (Banner of Truth, Edinburgh, 1970), p.81
[5] John Wesley, *The Works of Rev. John Wesley, A.M,* (HardPress Publishing, 2019), p.xix
[6] Bill Bradfield, *On Reading the Bible,* (Dover Publications Inc, 2005), p.81
[7] Eugene Peterson, *Eat this book,* (Hodder & Stoughton, London, 2006), p.15

'We open this book and find that page after page it takes us off guard, surprises us, and draws us into its reality, pulls us into participation with God on his terms.'[8]
Eugene Peterson

'Christians... will often feel that what God said to someone thousands of years ago speaks to their own condition so perfectly that it might have been written specially for them... The devotional maxim that one should read the Scriptures as one would read a personal letter from one's best friend rests not on pious fancy, but on the hardest theological fact.'
Jim Packer[9]

'There is one reason for reading the Bible, however, that is supreme: we read Scripture in order to encounter God there.'
Stephen J. Binz[10]

---

[8] Eugene Peterson, *Eat this book*, (Hodder & Stoughton, London, 2006), p.6
[9] J.I. Packer, *God has Spoken*, (Hodder & Stoughton, London, 1979), p.79
[10] Stephen J. Binz, *Conversing with God in Scripture,* (The Word Among Us Press, Maryland, 2008), p.13

Foreword

The Wardrobe is an excellent resource for any follower of Jesus who wants to anchor their faith more firmly in the truths of the Bible. The author has drawn from the depths of his experience and has poured out his pastoral heart, his theological training, and his love for the Scriptures and their Author, in order to provide his readers with a way into the treasure trove of God's Word. This book is for anyone who is seeking a reliable guide to the kingdom of heaven as revealed in the pages of the Bible.

Following the author into the 'Wardrobe of heaven' and into the depths of God's Word will enable the reader to plant their faith on the firmest of foundations, moving from a mere experiential knowledge of God, important though that is, to a firmly grounded theological grasp of the wonderful world of the kingdom of heaven. This book will serve as a reliable guide to understanding and exploring the Word of God and the kingdom which is revealed in its pages. As the author says, 'If we can learn to lean on this book ... if we have faith in this Word, we will hear the voice of God and sense His power working in our lives. If we do not believe and trust this Word, we will receive nothing but dead information.'

As you press into *The Wardrobe*, you will find not only that your understanding and grasp of Scripture will grow, but that you will develop 'depth, longevity, and a framework to your passion for the Lord' and so become a person who is filled both with the Word of God and the Spirit of God.

Every serious follower of Christ needs to come to a settled conviction as to what they believe, founded firmly on the Word of God. That is what this book will enable you to do if you are willing to push through and into the wonderful vistas of the kingdom that await. As Isaiah wrote: 'Your eyes will see the King in his beauty and view a land that stretches afar' (Isaiah 33:17). The door of this wardrobe is not locked. Adventure awaits. Press in!

Dr Robert Duerden.
January 2024.

Preface

I want to start this by retelling a well-known story. It is found in its original form in C.S. Lewis's book *The Magician's Nephew*. In the book, set in the magical and wonderful world of Narnia, a young lad called Digory is sent on a quest to find an apple from a garden located in the Western Wild. After a long and hard adventure, he brings the apple back to Aslan, the lion king of Narnia, knowing that this apple has healing properties, and thinking very much about his own seriously sick mother.

Aslan knew that Digory was thinking of his mother, and yet he told him to bury it into the soft mud by the riverbank. Digory struggled with this, but he did as he was instructed. After a difficult and mostly sleepless night, Digory awoke and quickly ran to the spot where he had buried the apple. In the morning light, he saw, to his wonder and surprise, there stood a magnificent and sweet-smelling apple tree. Aslan told Digory to pluck an apple from that tree, and then returned him, with the apple, to the world of men. When he arrived home, Digory ran up the stairs, quickly pared and cored the apple, and then fed it to his ailing mother. That evening, he took the peelings and the core and planted them at the bottom of the garden. The doctor came the next day and was amazed at her recovery.

Digory went out to the garden, and from the remains of that Narnian apple had sprung another magnificent apple tree, and it began to bear the most beautiful apples in the world, although they were not of quite the same quality as those found in Narnia itself.

One day something quite remarkable and strange happened. The sun was shining and there was a warm stillness in the air. Digory went out to the garden and to his astonishment, he saw the tree swaying as if being blown by a fierce wind. Lewis himself, describing this tree, wrote, 'But inside itself, in the very sap of it, the tree (so to speak) never forgot that other tree in Narnia to which it belonged. Sometimes it would move mysteriously when there was no wind blowing: I think that when this happened there were high winds in Narnia and the English tree quivered because, at that moment, the Narnian tree was rocking and swaying in a strong south-western gale.'[1]

I remember being profoundly moved to tears as I read that passage, and the cry of my heart rose to God saying that I would love to be like that English tree. Although it was deeply rooted in the soil of earth, it would somehow pick up and respond to movements that took place in Narnia. It spoke deeply to me and became a firm conviction that, although I was planted in the earth, I could become sensitive to the conversations and movements of heaven. I came to believe also that anyone who gives serious and loving attention to the Word of God, putting down deep roots into the life of God shall also

---

[1] C.S. Lewis, *The Magician's Nephew*, (Grafton, London, 2002), p.170

be like that tree, rooted and sensitive to the words and activities of heaven.

Many years later, the tree blew down in a large storm. Digory, now a middle-aged professor, could not bear to have it cut into firewood, and so he had it built into a wardrobe. Lewis wrote, 'and although he himself did not discover the magical properties of that wardrobe, someone else did. And that was the beginnings of all the comings and goings between Narnia and our world.'[2]

That 'someone else' was a young girl called Lucy, who one day found herself stumbling into the world of Narnia whilst hiding in that wardrobe.

The Bible, like the Narnian wardrobe, can become the wardrobe of heaven, leading to vistas of God and His kingdom. If we enter in, pushing through, we will find ourselves tumbling into this wonderful world of the kingdom of heaven. We must learn to go there often and explore the terrain.

---

[2] C.S. Lewis, *The Magician's Nephew*, (Grafton, London, 2002), p.171

INTRODUCTION

When I was a child, my parents would occasionally take us on holiday to a small hamlet called Lothersdale. It was a small community, comprising of around 200 houses, nestled in the North Yorkshire hills. We would spend the whole day travelling nearly 300 miles from our home in Littlehampton in Sussex, in an old Ford Prefect. Once there, we would spend two glorious weeks with my mother's sister, her husband and their two daughters.

Central to the village was the Dale End Mill, otherwise known as Lothersdale Mill. Its history goes back into the 16th century. It was first used for grinding the local corn and then converted into a textile mill. It is still a historic building in North Yorkshire, housing a magnificent suspension wheel, forty-five feet in diameter. In fact, it had the reputation of being the largest indoor waterwheel in the world.

Over the years, our Yorkshire family had 'adopted' an elderly gentleman called Tom, who was a widower. He lived in the village, and he became 'Grandad Tom' to us. He often ate dinner with us and, later in the evenings, he would tell us bedtime stories. My fondest memory of him was of a day when I was a little reluctant to eat my meal. Grandad Tom gently leaned over towards me and said in my ear, *'Gerrit it down tha' neck, lad.'* I have often used that saying to each of my five children over the years, and I'm sure they have passed it on.

Grandad Tom has long gone, but his pithy little saying has never left me. In fact, it was almost prophetic. Many years later, at the age of 20, I became a Christian and a friend's dad put a Bible into my hand. And so began my journey of reading this old book. It seemed so big, so long, so old. But I persevered. It was not always easy, but I stuck at it, and there came times when, like Lucy in the wardrobe, I felt myself being drawn into another world which, I began to discover, was the world of the kingdom of heaven.

If you feel the Bible is too complicated or difficult, then I simply want to say to you, 'Gerrit it down tha' neck.' I want to encourage, prompt, and stir you to get into the Bible, and to let it get into you. Keep at it, and you will begin to feel the nourishment. You will also become increasingly aware of God's kingdom and what is going on there, for, 'reading is an immense gift, but only if the words are assimilated, taken into the soul – eaten, gnawed, received in unhurried delight.'[1]

In the prophecy of Ezekiel, we find written these words:

> And he said to me, 'Son of man, eat whatever you find here. Eat this scroll, and go, speak to the house of Israel.' So I opened my mouth, and he gave me this scroll to eat. And he said to me, 'Son of man, feed your belly with this scroll that I give you and fill your

---

[1] Eugene Peterson, *Eat this book*, (Hodder & Stoughton, London, 2006), p.11

stomach with it.' Then I ate it, and it was in my mouth as sweet as honey (Ezekiel 3:1–3).

Jeremiah, a contemporary of Ezekiel, wrote, 'Your words were found, and I ate them, and your words became to me a joy and the delight of my heart, for I am called by your name, O LORD, God of hosts' (Jeremiah 15:16).

In the book of Revelation, the aged apostle John had a conversation with the angel about a scroll. He records, 'So I went to the angel and told him to give me the little scroll. And he said to me, "Take and eat it; it will make your stomach bitter, but in your mouth it will be sweet as honey"' (Revelation 10:9).

Eugene Peterson, writing about John, said, 'He eats the book – not just reads it – he got it into his nerve endings, his reflexes, his imagination.'[2] I would like you to learn to do the same.

---

[2] Eugene Peterson, *Eat this book*, (Hodder & Stoughton, London, 2006), p.9

Chapter 1

Where Did the Bible Come From?

On the morning of 6th October 1536, William Tyndale, the Bible translator, was taken from his place of imprisonment within Vilvoorde Castle in Antwerp and led into the public square to be executed. There he was tied to a stake, strangled, and then his body was burned. His last words reportedly were: 'Oh Lord, open the King of England's eyes.' He had been convicted of heresy, and that supposed heresy was translating the whole of the New Testament and parts of the Old Testament into the English language from both the Hebrew and Greek manuscripts. His desire was to get the Bible into the hands of ordinary men and women.

Ironically, two years later, King Henry VIII authorised the publication of the *Great Bible* for the Church of England, of which most of the New Testament had been the work of Tyndale himself.

As we pick up and hold our own Bibles in our hands, we need to realise that we are holding a remarkable, and might I say, a costly book. Over the centuries, men like William Tyndale have suffered and died in order that we might have the freedom not only to own one, but to be able to read it for ourselves.

The Bible has not gone out of date. It is not a relic from the past that has been relegated to numerous second-hand bookshops all over the world. The very opposite is true. The Bible is very much alive and kicking!

According to *Guinness World Records*, the Bible is still the top seller. On their website, it reads, 'Although it is impossible to obtain exact figures, there is little doubt that the Bible is the world's best-selling and most widely distributed book.'[1]

The Bible Society records that 50 Bibles are still being sold every minute![2]

In December 2019, the United Kingdom saw the start of Covid-19. Over the next few years, over 66,000 people in Great Britain lost their lives to the disease, with an estimated seven million deaths world-wide.[3] During that awful time, many began searching for deep answers. In April 2020, the *New Statesman* reported, 'The top English-language Bible on Google Play and App Store was installed almost two million times, the highest amount ever recorded for March, according to *Appfigures*. Similarly, one of the UK's largest online Christian bookstores, Eden, saw physical Bible sales rise by 55 per cent.'[4]

Personally, I was twenty years old when I was given my first Bible. It was on Sunday morning, 30 March 1969. I had become

---

[1] http://www.guinnessworldrecords.com/world-records/best-selling-book-of-non-fiction/
[2] https://www.biblesociety.org.uk/latest/news/bible-distributing-breaks-record-for-2014/
[3] https://www.worldometers.info/coronavirus/coronavirus-death-toll/
[4] https://www.newstatesman.com/politics/religion/2020/04/how-coronavirus-leading-religious-revival

a Christian four days earlier. It was something I had never seen before, and it looked a bit daunting. So, I started at the beginning, and after a while, I was hooked! Since then, I have gone through and worn out several Bibles, but I still have most of them in my library.

There is something about this book – the Bible – that has a drawing power. Over the centuries both men and women, boys and girls, have turned to the Scriptures, and have found not only hope and comfort, warnings and direction, but they have also begun to hear the voice of God for themselves. They have felt themselves being drawn into God's big story.

Here in the West many people have numerous Bibles, often in different translations and paraphrases. We also have easy access to the Bible and Bible resources on the internet. Sadly, for many, the Bible is so easily accessible and taken for granted, that it has moved from being a lifeline to an occasional resource for finding the keys for successful living.

In the early 1970s, as a young Christian on a mission team in the South of France, I was introduced to the writings of Aiden Wilson Tozer (1897–1963). His effect on my life was profound. In my view, his books have the sharpness of a prophetic edge, the depths of long meditation in the Scriptures, the results of much prayerfulness, all of which disturb us out of a spiritual stupor and point us towards a serious walk with the living God. His books are collectables, ageless and re-readable in their messages and deserve pride of place in any library. He wrote, 'The Bible is not an end in itself, but a means to bring men to an intimate and satisfying knowledge of God, that they may enter into him, that they may delight in his presence, may taste and know the inner sweetness of the very God himself in the core and centre of their hearts.'[5]

My desire is to inspire you to take the Bible seriously. I want you to understand just how important it is in shaping the life, not only of the church, but also of the individual. This is no ordinary book. *Caveat lector* – 'let the reader beware' – it could, and should, change your life.

I invite you to travel with me through the pages of this book. In it we will look at the origins of the Bible and its journey to being in your possession. We will also consider the place it should have in our lives, and the deep and long-term effect it will have in us, as we start giving it our full attention. We will look at some technical stuff, some inspirational stuff and some very practical stuff.

The result should be a renewed love, a deep respect and a persistent passion for these ancient Scriptures. My hope is that the Bible will become a book you will resort to easily, often and longingly.

Where Did the Bible Come From?

So, to make a start. Where did the Bible come from? Did it drop out of the sky? Did someone find it in a box hidden inside a cave? Did an angel come down from heaven and present it to someone? The truth of the matter is that the Bible is both a very human and a powerfully supernatural story. The Bible we have today is the result of hundreds of years of collating ancient writings.

---

[5] A.W. Tozer, *The Pursuit of God*, (Kingsway Publications, 1982), p.10

This collection of sacred writings was written by around 40 different writers, from a variety of social and cultural backgrounds, yet all of them were inspired by God the Holy Spirit to write over a period of approximately 1500 years.

As the apostle Peter wrote, 'No prophecy of Scripture comes from someone's own interpretation. For no prophecy was ever produced by the will of man, but men spoke from God *as they were carried along by the Holy Spirit*' (2 Peter 1:21; emphasis mine). God was breathing out these words into the minds of men.

Mostly, I suspect, they were not conscious of this supernatural intervention. In their minds, they were simply writing prayers, narratives, poetry and recording prophecies. Sometimes they felt inspired under a prophetic anointing; at other times, they were recording the results of thorough research. Yet somehow the hand of God was on it all, and years later, their writings would be recognised as bearing the distinct authority of God's voice.

The *New Bible Dictionary* says, 'Scripture has a double authorship, and man is only the secondary author. The Primary Author, through Whose initiative and prompting and enlightenment, and under Whose superintendence each human writer did his work, is God the Holy Spirit.'[6]

Messianic Rabbi Glenn Harris is the Pastor of Congregation Shema Yisrael in Birmingham, Michigan. In an essay entitled *Can I trust the Bible*, he wrote about trying to imagine forty different people from different periods of time, and from

---

[6] James Packer, *Inspiration, New Bible Dictionary,* (Inter-Varsity Press, London, 1970), pp.564,565

various backgrounds and cultures, all coming up with something that, when put together, spoke of the same story and had a remarkable harmony to it.[7] This extraordinary compendium of books tells the story of God's persistent and redemptive pursuit of humanity.

There are 66 books in the Bible. The Old Testament contains 39 books, and the New Testament contains 27 books. Despite the diversity of authors, it contains this one unifying theme of God's compassionate, persistent and redemptive pursuit of humanity.

The Bible is a Translation

When we look at the Bible in our hands, we need to realise, firstly, that we are holding a translation. The Old Testament books were written mainly in Hebrew, with a little bit of Aramaic thrown in, and the New Testament was written in a basic Greek dialect first used by the armies of Alexander the Great. It was called *koinē* (pronounced koy-nay) Greek and it was the common language. It is largely unused today, but still utilised by Greek Orthodox Churches in their liturgical services.

The Hebrew of Psalm 23:1 looks like this (Hebrew is read backwards):

מִזְמוֹר לְדָוִד: יְהוָה רֹעִי, לֹא אֶחְסָר

The *koinē* Greek of John 3:16 looks like this:

---

[7] Rabbi Glenn Harris, *Can I Trust the Bible?*, retrieved from https://www.gospeloutreach.net/bible.html

Οὕτως γὰρ ἠγάπησεν ὁ θ ε ὸς τὸν κόσμον ὥστε τὸν υἱὸν αὐτοῦ τὸν μονογενῆ ἔδωκεν ἵνα πᾶς ὁ πιστεύων εἰς αὐτὸν μὴ ἀπόληται ἀλλ' ἔχῃ ζ ω ὴν αἰώνιον

As we have noted, the books and letters that make up the Bible were written a very long time ago. The original parchments are no longer extant (they no longer exist). These originals have been called by the literary experts 'autographs,' and unfortunately, there are no 'autographed' copies existing today. They have been lost to us.

What we do have today, however, are very precise copies, and lots of them. In fact, the Jewish people were so meticulous in the copying of the manuscripts, that they would count the words, the sentences, and the paragraphs. They would even count the Hebrew punctuation marks – 'jots' and 'tittles' – or as they were otherwise called, 'iotas' and 'little marks.'

The word 'Bible' came from the Latin word *biblica*, and the Greek word *biblia*. These words simply means 'the books.' From within the New Testament, this collection of Old Testament books was also called 'prophetic writings' (Romans 16:26), 'sacred writings' (2 Timothy 3:15) or Scriptures' (mentioned 19 times). It is also interesting to note that for the early church the Bible was in fact the Old Testament. Jesus, the apostles, and Paul all read from the Old Testament. The letters and the gospels had not yet been written!

The apostle Paul wrote to Timothy, 'All Scripture is *breathed out by God and profitable for teaching, for reproof, for correction, and for training in righteousness*' (2 Timothy 3:16;

emphasis mine). It is my belief that it was these original manuscripts – these 'autographs' – that were inspired.

James Packer wrote, 'Paul's words mean, not that Scripture is inspiring (true though this is), but that Scripture is a divine product, and must be approached and estimated as such.'[8]

However, for centuries, and especially during the time of the (so-called) Enlightenment, the truths and authenticity of the Bible have been questioned.

Bernard Ramm, a Professor of Philosophy and Systematic Theology, concurred:

> A thousand times over, the death knell of the Bible has been sounded, the funeral procession formed, the inscription cut on the tombstone, and committal read. But somehow the corpse never stays put. No other book has been so chopped, knifed, sifted, scrutinized, and vilified. What book on philosophy or religion or psychology or *belles lettres* [beautiful letters] of classical or modern times has been subject to such a mass attack as the Bible? With such venom and scepticism? With such thoroughness and erudition? Upon every chapter, line and tenet?[9]

So, what is it about the Bible that has resulted in it being so viciously attacked over the years?

The main reason, in my opinion, is that the Bible speaks liberating and healing words of truth, but there is a powerful

---

[8] James Packer, *Inspiration, New Bible Dictionary*, (Inter-Varsity Press, London, 1970), p.564
[9] Bernard Ramm, *Protestant Christian Evidences*, (Moody Press, Chicago, 1953), pp. 232-233

spiritual enemy who is dedicated to distorting and ridiculing the Bible in order to keep people bound in darkness.

The Manuscripts

It is commonly agreed that the older the manuscripts, the more precise and accurate they will be. Until the 1940s, the oldest known Old Testament manuscripts, written in Hebrew, dated from the ninth and tenth century AD. They were copies of the Pentateuch, the first five books of the Old Testament, and they were about 1000 years old. There were others, but not quite that old.

This all changed quite dramatically between 1947 and 1956. During this period, a remarkable discovery of ancient scrolls was made, hidden and preserved inside clay pots, in caves near the site of the Qumran Community by the Dead Sea. They became known as 'The Dead Sea Scrolls.' They were, in fact, a collection of 972 texts from the Hebrew Bible, along with some extra-biblical documents. When these manuscripts and fragments were examined, they were dated between 150 BC and AD 70. Their discovery was an amazing find for biblical scholars. The Isaiah scroll, for example, predated all other copies by about 1000 years! The longest scroll was about 28 feet in length. Imagine laying that out in your front room.

It needs to be said that there are far more copies of the Scriptures than there are of any other ancient writings. For example, there are only ten copies of the writings of Julius Caesar and seven copies of the writings of Plato, whereas there are 972 copies of the Old Testament and 5,664 copies of the New Testament.

It's also interesting to know that it is theoretically possible to reconstruct the whole of the New Testament from the writings of the early Church Fathers (AD 100–450) [10].

Copies of the Scriptures

Until Johannes Gutenburg first printed the Latin Bible in 1456, all Bibles had been hand-copied onto papyrus, parchment and paper. The oldest existing Greek translations of the Old Testament are the *Chester Beatty Papyri* (discovered in 1931) containing nine Old Testament books. These date between AD 200–250. Near to that, we have the *Codex Vaticanus* and the *Codex Sinaiticus*, both of which are Greek translations of the Old and New Testaments, and both contain almost all the books of the Old Testament. They date around AD 350. The earliest Greek manuscript is the Rylands Papyrus, containing a portion of John's Gospel (John 18:31–33,37). It was found in Egypt, and dates around AD 125–130.

At this point, we need to mention the variants. These are the slight differences and variations in wording among the thousands of copied manuscripts that we have today. Gordon Fee, Professor of New Testament at Regent College, Vancouver, felt that the variants were either accidental slips or deliberate attempts by the copyist to 'improve' the text by making it more understandable.[11] Conservative theologians will say that the existing (extant) copies we have, with all the variants, contain 99% of the original text.

---

[10] See J.H. Greenlee, *Introduction To New Testament Textual Criticism*, (Baker Academic, Revised ed. Edition, 1993), p.54
[11] Gordon Fee, *New Testament Exegesis*, (Westminster John Knox Press, Kentucky, 2002), p.60

It is also worth noting that the chapter and verse divisions that are found in our modern Bibles were not inspired, and they are not found in any of the ancient manuscripts. Chapter divisions were introduced by Bishop Stephen Langton in 1228, and verse divisions were added by Rabbi Nathan in 1448. They are helpful at times, but on many occasions, they can break the flow of what the writer was saying.

The Old Testament Writings

The Old Testament Scriptures can be divided into four different sections: the Torah, the Historical Books, the Prophets and the Writings.

The Torah is the collective name of the first five books of the Bible, written by Moses, consisting of Genesis, Exodus, Leviticus, Numbers and Deuteronomy. It is also called the Pentateuch, taken from a Greek word meaning 'five-volumed.' In our Bibles, the Hebrew *tôrâh* is translated as 'the Law'. *Tôrâh* comes from the root word *yârâh*, which means 'to throw or to shoot.' These books could be considered the javelin words of God that target, pierce and instruct human hearts and minds.

All the teachings of the Bible find their beginnings here in these first five books. The whole of the Torah is constructed around the 'Ten Words' – what we know as the Ten Commandments. The account of their giving is found in Deuteronomy 5:5–21.

Furthermore, according to Jesus, these Ten Words were built on two commandments. Matthew records a conversation between Him and a religious lawyer: 'And one of them, a lawyer, asked him a question to test him. "Teacher, which is the great commandment in the Law?" And he said to him, "You shall love the Lord your God with all your heart and with all your soul and with all your mind. This is the great and first commandment. And a second is like it: You shall love your neighbour as yourself. On these two commandments depend all the Law and the Prophets'" (Matthew 22:34–40). This can be further reduced to: 'Love God, love people.'

In a lecture given in 1978, a certain Dr Donald G. Miller, outlined the thrust of the first five books of the Bible.[12] I have summarised them as follows:

Genesis was Israel's conception. It reveals the prenatal Word of God. Everything within these pages is embryonic. A cosmos, a world and a nation were conceived here. It is worth noting that all the great doctrines of the Bible have their seedbed here. Most possibly, this is the reason why this book has been so viciously attacked by the sceptics and the anti-supernaturalists over the centuries.

Exodus was Israel's birth and infancy. The long pregnancy brought forth the people of God. There was a painful labour in Egypt, the waters broke at the Red Sea, and then the newborn nation stood, a little shaky, on the other shore. They were then taken through the wilderness to Mount Sinai, where they learned their first words – the Ten Words – the Ten Commandments.

Leviticus was Israel's childhood and schooling. In the journey through the wilderness, the infant nation learned to walk carefully and closely with God. There were lots of visual things to look at like sacrifices and special garments.

---

[12] As referenced by Eugene Peterson, *Working the Angles*, (Eerdmans, 1987), pp.59-61

Numbers was Israel's adolescence. The young nation awkwardly flexed its muscles and started kicking against the goads. They grumbled and rebelled against the old establishment of Moses and Aaron.

Deuteronomy was Israel's adulthood. The people of God matured into a life of faith, and having been well educated and tested, they stood on the verge of the Jordan, ready to enter the Promised Land.

Interestingly, in Psalm 119:18 King David prayed, 'Open my eyes, that I may behold wondrous things out of your law.' The very 'law' he spoke about was these five books of Moses. There are, therefore, for the hungry seeker after God, many wonderful things to be found in these five books.

Following the Torah come the **Historical Books**. These books recount the story of Israel's entry into the Promised Land under Joshua; Israel's life under the judges; Israel's transition into kingship under Samuel; the dividing of the kingdom after Solomon into Judah and Samaria; the downfall of both Samaria and Judah; Israel's life under Exile and Israel's return from Exile.

Mingled into this history were the **Prophets**. These were the writings of men who somehow had incredible access to the throne, the ear and the voice of God. They were able to see what He was up to and clearly hear His words. Bravely, they spoke of what they had seen and heard to an erring nation, who really did not want to listen or respond. Originally, they were divided into the former prophets (Joshua, Judges, Samuel, Kings) and the latter prophets (Isaiah, Jeremiah, Ezekiel and 'the book of the 12 prophets').

Finally, there were **the Writings**. Some of them were also called 'wisdom' literature. These generally fell into three areas: Firstly, the Psalms, Proverbs and Job. Secondly, 'the five scrolls' – The Song of Solomon, Ruth, Lamentations, Ecclesiastes, and Esther. Thirdly, Daniel, Ezra-Nehemiah and Chronicles.

Eugene Peterson wrote of this first group that:

> Sometimes these responses are argumentative as in Job, sometimes wise reflections as in Proverbs, but mostly they are prayer as in the Psalms. The Psalms dominate the writings and provide the major documentation for what it means to answer 'out of the depth' the God who addresses His people.[13]

Scripture itself makes mention of the existence of collections of authorised books. (Exodus 24:4-7 / Deuteronomy 31:24-26 / Joshua 1:8 / 2 Kings 22:8-11 / Nehemiah 8:1) By 300 BC, there were 'the Scriptures' which contained the Law, the Prophets, and the Writings.

The prophet Daniel referred to 'the books' and, in this case, he was speaking of the early prophetic writings. Daniel wrote, 'In the first year of Darius the son of Ahasuerus, by descent a Mede, who was made king over the realm of the Chaldeans – in the first year of his reign, I, Daniel, perceived in the books the number of years that, according to the word of the LORD to Jeremiah the prophet, must pass before the end of the desolations of Jerusalem, namely, seventy years' (Daniel 9:1,2).

Details of the final compilation of the Old Testament books and writings are not known, but reliable tradition tells us that

---

[13] Eugene Peterson, *Working the Angles*, (Eerdmans, 1987), pp.54,55

it happened after Israel's return from Exile in around 500 BC. Certainly, in the New Testament there are quotations from all but four of the 39 books of the Old Testament.

The books of the Apocrypha, found in the Jerusalem Bible, have no divine authority about them, but 1 and 2 Maccabees are a pretty reliable historical source for the 400-year gap between the two Testaments.

Around the third century BC, there came the emergence of the Septuagint, which was a Greek version of the Hebrew Old Testament. The word Septuagint arose from the Latin, *versio septuaginta interpretum*, which meant 'translation of the seventy interpreters.' Its precise origins are still being debated, but it is certain that the work was started in Alexandria in the reign of Ptolemy Philadelphus (285–246 BC), for the benefit of the Greek-speaking Jews who lived there.

It became the Bible of the New Testament era and was used extensively by Jesus and the apostles. This explains why there are some differences found between Old Testament texts and how they are quoted in the New Testament. It is like comparing the King James Version with the New International Version.

The Jewish Bible is structured around three sections: Torah (the Law, also known as the first five books of Moses or the Pentateuch), the Prophets and the Writings. Our English Old Testament is structured slightly differently into five sections: Torah, the Historical books, the Wisdom books, the Major prophets and the Minor prophets. The categorisations 'major' and 'minor' in regard to the prophets have nothing to do with importance, but rather are to do with the lengths of the books.

The New Testament Writings

These writings, as seen in the New Testament of today, are arranged into four divisions. Firstly, the four Gospels, which are accounts of the life and ministry of Jesus. This is then followed by the book of Acts, written by Luke, describing the birth and growth of the early church. Thirdly, we have the Letters, written by apostles and apostolic men, to various churches and individuals. Lastly, there is the Revelation, an apocalyptic book written by the apostle John.

The bringing together and arranging of this collection took around 300 years, and for 1,600 years now, most Christians have accepted the current 27 books. The whole process looked something like this:

The Oral Tradition. These were 'the words of the Lord Jesus' (Acts 20:35 / 1 Corinthians 11:23 onwards). We must remember that Jesus did not write a book. In fact, during His earthly life, it's likely nothing of what He said and did was written down; everything was remembered, spoken, and passed on. This was in the period AD 30–50.

The Letters and Gospels, written roughly between AD 50–100. It is interesting to note that all of Paul's letters were written and in circulation before the first Gospel was written.

The Distribution of these Writings. They were circulated, collected and read in the churches (AD 100–200).

There was also a plethora of other writings around this time, from peripheral and fringe sects. These were carefully examined and compared with the Letters and the Gospels, and it was quickly seen which were authentic, and which were obviously spurious (AD 200–300).

Complete agreement was eventually attained around AD 300–400, albeit through much prayer, much discussion and several meetings of various councils.

The Canons of Scripture

We now need to look at this word 'canon'. It comes from the Greek word *kanōn* which means 'a measuring rod, a ruler'. When it came to both the Old and New Testament writings, there was a double meaning to the process. A measuring rod has first to be measured and constructed. Then it measures all that is brought to it. In the same way, these books, thoroughly tested over many years by godly theologians and scholars, became the rule by which all other writings were tested. The canons of both Testaments also became the rule of thumb, as it were, for living a godly life.

What, then, set the standard for this measuring rod? And by what grounds were these books recognised as inspired? There was a threefold test that was set:

- The authority of the writers. The Old Testament was written by the lawgivers and the prophets. The New Testament, by the apostles and their immediate associates.
- The unanimous decisions. There was a remarkable unanimity over their authority.
- The internal evidence. Within all the writings, the same three things were noticed:
  1. **Sound, pure doctrine and teaching** were found in all the books – there was complete conformity and consistency of truth.
  2. They were all **self-authenticating**. There was, in fact, a deep and strong authority about them. Being part of the

canon did not give them authority; they were in the canon because of their authority. No human council gave them authority; they merely recognised the authority they had.

T.C. Hammond, in his super little book, *In Understanding Be Men*, wrote:

> The spiritual discernment imparted to the Christians almost instinctively recognised and acknowledged the divine inspiration of the scriptural books. It is only the Holy Spirit's witness that produces a true spiritual persuasion of their spiritual authority. The voice of the Spirit in the Scripture answers to the voice of the Spirit in the Christian.[14]

Similarly, the Belgian Confession, written in 1561, says in Article 5, 'And we believe without a doubt all things contained in them – not so much because the church receives and approves them as such but above all because the Holy Spirit testifies in our hearts that they are from God, and also because they prove themselves to be from God.'[15]

3. They had enjoyed **continuous acceptance and usage** by the church at large. For over 1,500 years, the church has believed and taught from these recognised books. And this canon of Scripture – our Bible – has worked with

---

[14] T.C. Hammond, *In Understanding be Men*, (Inter-Varsity Press, Leicester, 1977), pp.30,31
[15] Retrieved from https://www.crcna.org/welcome/beliefs/confessions/belgic-confession

transformative power in the hearts and minds of men and women throughout the ages.

A History of Translations

The Aramaic Targums. A 'Targum' is literally 'a translation, an interpretation'. They were free 'paraphrastic' (the expressing of the meaning by other words – paraphrase) renderings of the Hebrew Scriptures into Aramaic. They start to appear around the last century BC and the middle of the first century AD. The early church would have had access to these.

The Syriac Peshitta. The spread of Christianity into Syria brought about the need for a translation in their own language. The word 'Peshitta' literally means 'simple version'.

The Latin Vulgate (The Common version). This was produced around the time the Eastern church was splitting from the Western church. It is attributed to Jerome, who at the request of Pope Damasus for 'an authentic and standard authorised version' commenced his labours in AD 382. His rendering of the Old Testament is quite a free translation. However, 'this translation proved to be to the West what the Septuagint had been to the East, that it was prepared with great care by the greatest scholar whom Latin Christianity produced, that it was for hundreds of years the only Bible in universal use in Europe.'[16]

Wycliffe Bible. This version was completed in 1384 and written in the everyday speech of the common people. It was translated from the Latin Vulgate into the Middle English of the day (a

---

[16] *The International Standard Bible Encyclopaedia,* e-sword.net

form of the English language that was spoken after the Norman Conquest of 1066, until the late 15th century).

Tyndale's Bible. This was started in 1526 with a translation of the New Testament. Tyndale was the first to use the available Hebrew and Greek manuscripts in addition to the Latin Vulgate. Many of his copies were burned by the Bishop of London. Again, it was written in the modern idiom. For example, the opening words of Paul's letter to Titus reads, 'Paul, the rascal of God and the villein of Jesus Christ' (Titus 1:1).

Coverdale's Bible. This was completed in 1535 with many assistants. It was not a labour of love, but a task imposed upon him by Oliver Cromwell. Neither was it from the original, but from the German and Latin versions, and bore the marks of 'haste and carelessness.'

Geneva Bible. This was produced by Protestant exiles during the reign of Queen Mary (1553–1558). By 1611, about 150 copies had appeared. Copies are still to be found. It has been affectionately called the 'Breeches Bible' because of the way it renders Genesis 3:7: 'they sewed figge tree leaves together and made themselves breeches.'

King James Bible. It has been called 'the noblest monument of English prose.' In 1604, King James ordered a new translation. Many scholars were put into six groups: two at Oxford, two at Cambridge and two at Westminster. The work started in 1607 and was finished in 1611. The scholars used the best versions and available manuscripts.

Revised Bible. Published 20 June 1885, this version was entrusted to over 50 scholars from various denominations and was a revision of the original King James Version to account for updated language and scholarship. Here I quote from the preface to the Revised Standard Version: 'The King James version has grave defects. By the middle of the 19th century, the development of biblical studies and the discovery of many manuscripts more ancient than those upon which the King James version was based, made it manifest that these defects are so many and so serious as to call for a revision of the English translation...the KJV of the New Testament was based upon a Greek text that was marred by mistakes.'[17] About 2,000 to be precise! 1 John 5:7 in the KJV is a spurious verse. It was inserted by Vigilius around AD 500 and technically called 'a pious fraud'. Also, today, many of the words are archaic and obsolete.

Revised Standard Version. This was published on 12 September 1952. 32 scholars worked together on the best manuscripts available.

New American Standard Bible. The complete Bible published in 1971. It became probably the most literal translation of the Bible of its time.

New International Version. Having its beginnings in 1965, this translation was made by over 100 scholars, each book assigned to a team. The whole Bible was published in 1978.

English Standard Version. This was completed in 2001, by a team of over 100 biblical and textual scholars led by J.I. Packer, Professor of Theology at Regents College, Vancouver. This, in my view, is probably one of the most accurate versions of the Old and New Testaments to date.

---

[17] Preface to the *Revised Standard Version*, (Oxford University Press, London, 1952), pp.iii,vi

Translations and Paraphrases

A paraphrase is not strictly a translation. There are three terms used in the world of Bible translations that we should familiarise ourselves with.

Speaking of translations, the first term is *essentially literal*. This is a 'word for word' translation of the ancient manuscripts into our current language. I would place the New American Standard Bible and the English Standard Version in this category.

The second term is *dynamic equivalence*. This is a 'thought for thought' translation – not strictly literal but conveying accurately the thought processes of the original author. I would place the New International Version into this category.

When we talk about the third term, *paraphrase*, these are 'heart to heart' translations that go beyond the second term. They will give the heart and the spirit of what has been written, but certainly not the exact meaning of each word and phrase. There are many which are excellent for introducing young Christians to the Bible. Among them I would list the J.B. Phillips New Testament, the Weymouth New Testament, the Living Bible, the Good News Bible and the Message.

Falling in between the second and third term is the New Living Translation. In the 'Note to Readers' section to this version the publishers wrote, 'The New Living Translation is based on the most recent scholarship in the theory of translation...translating entire thoughts (rather than just words) into natural, everyday English. The result is a translation that is easy to read and understand and that accurately communicates the meaning of the original text.'[18]

Having waded through all these details, let me sum up by saying that the Bible is not so much a book to be admired, read and even memorised, but a book to be heard and absorbed. We need to learn to read the Bible, listening for the true and authentic voice of God that is to be found within its pages. We should be aware of its history and the type of translation we are reading, to inform our hearts and minds in Christ Jesus.

We come to this book then, not only to read and understand the vast story of God, but to listen deeply to His living voice. As we make ourselves available in giving our attention to the Bible, God will speak life, truth, wisdom and understanding into our hearts.

Three Important Personal Influences

Let me finish this chapter by referring to three historical characters who have always been an inspiration to me.

The first one is George Müller (1805–1898). He founded several orphanages in Bristol. He was a man who loved the Scriptures and prayer. He was affectionately nicknamed the 'apostle of faith', because in his personal prayer journal he recorded over 20,000 direct answers to prayer. He died when he was about 93, having read the whole Bible over 200 times from cover to cover. It is well worth reading his biography, written by Arthur T. Pierson. This begs the question: Where does faith come from? The apostle Paul wrote, 'Faith comes from hearing, and hearing through the words of Christ' (Romans 10:17).

---

[18] A Note to Readers, *New Living Translation*, (Tyndale House Publishers, Illinois, 1996)

Müller's mind and heart were saturated by the word of God, and deep faith was born and nurtured within him.

The second character is C.T. Studd (1860–1931). He was converted from a very wealthy background. He was also a professional cricketer, playing for England in the memorable match won by Australia in 1882, which brought about the creation of 'The Ashes'. After his conversion, he gave away his inheritance (then £29,000 and now worth just under £2.5 million) left to him by his late father, and became a missionary, first to China, then India and finally Africa. As an old man in Africa, he would rise around five o'clock each morning to read the Bible for about two hours. His ministry during the day would come out of those encounters with the Scriptures.

The third character is Professor Ralph Shallis (1912–1986). A Bible teacher who used to speak often at missionary training conferences, Ralph would tithe his day to God, giving Him and the Scriptures his full attention for over two and a half hours each day. He would also read the Scriptures in their original languages. I recall walking into the library of the OM (Operation Mobilisation) headquarters in Paris to see Ralph poring over the pages of his Bible, with his coloured pencils arranged like a rainbow around it. I am still inspired by that memory.

Ralph was a great help to me personally. He said to me one day, 'Alan, you know I have so many young people coming to me, propounding their favourite and pet doctrines. To be honest, I will not even listen to them. In fact, I will not listen until they have read the complete Bible from cover to cover at least thirteen times. I do not see how they can be convinced until they have done so.'

These words floored me. I felt at that point that I hadn't even started! Over the years since that startling conversation, I've come to see that he was perfectly right.

Ralph gave me time, mentoring me for a while, and instilled in my heart a deep desire to know and understand the Scriptures. That desire has never left me.

The first Psalm says, 'Blessed is the man who walks not in the counsel of the wicked, nor stands in the way of sinners, nor sits in the seat of scoffers; but his delight is in the law of the LORD, and on his law, he meditates day and night. He is like a tree planted by streams of water that yields its fruit in its season, and its leaf does not wither. In all that he does, he prospers' (Psalm 1:1–3).

Chapter 2

Can I Trust the Bible?

A Philosophical Context

What and how we think about the Bible is very important. How we read the Bible is also very important. If we feel it's only a large collection of ancient writings, then it will remain quite dusty and lifeless to us. If we do not trust it, we will never hear the voice of God in it. Faith is intrinsic to our reading of, and receiving from, the Scriptures.

The writer to the Hebrews wrote of those who had difficulty receiving the Word of God. He declared that 'The message they heard did not benefit them, because they were not united by faith with those who listened' (Hebrews 4:2). I particularly like the rendition of this text in the Good News Bible. 'They heard the message, but it did them no good, because when they heard it, *they did not accept it with faith*' (emphasis mine). Dr John Brown of Edinburgh (1784–1858) wrote, 'It is by believing a principle that it becomes influential, as it is by digesting food that it becomes nutritive.'[1]

The writer to the Hebrews expounded on this a few verses later: 'For the word of God is *living and active*, sharper than any two-edged sword, piercing to the division of soul and of spirit, of joints and of marrow, and discerning the thoughts and intentions of the heart' (Hebrews 4:12; emphasis mine).

To the one reading and listening with the ears and heart of faith, the Bible becomes 'living and active', and begins to transform us. On the other hand, to an unbelieving, distrustful heart, the Bible contains mere lifeless words on a page. In a nutshell, if we do not trust this book, we will never hear the voice of God speaking through it.

If we are honest, distrust comes to us far more easily than trust. In our Western culture, we are conditioned to be suspicious, ask questions and not take things at face value. In one sense, that is good advice, but lurking beneath is a darker philosophy. Let me explain.

We have been (and still are in many areas of our thinking and practice) living through a 'postmodern era' of thought and philosophy. In a positive sense, this epoch in history has been characterised by a desire for community, an appreciation of dialogue and an openness to fresh ideas. On the darker side, it has introduced a plethora of negative attitudes, such as an aversion to absolutes, a distrust of text, an insistence on relativity, problems with authority, difficulties with choices, an aversion to long-term commitments, a disturbing vagueness on theological truths and a haziness regarding moral and ethical

---

[1] John Brown, *Hebrews*, (Banner of Truth, Edinburgh, 1976), p.204

issues. Its implications into how truth is taught have been significant and it's also gone far in eroding several ancient Christian teachings and practices.

At the very roots of postmodernism are the writings of Friedrich Nietzsche (1844–1900), dubbed the 'patron saint' of postmodern philosophy. In his writings, he insisted that God was dead. Writing to a friend in 1883, Nietzsche described himself as 'the antichrist' and 'the most terrible opponent of Christianity.'[2] He was an aggressive atheist.

In his books, he propounded and developed what was called 'a hermeneutic of suspicion,'[3] where suspicion must shape the interpretation of everything we hear and read. This way of thinking has penetrated deeply into our learning processes.

Nietzsche felt that to have settled convictions about anything was dangerous. All knowledge, to him, was merely a matter of personal perspective. He insisted that how we *personally* see and understand things becomes the *truth* of the matter, and those views are always open to readjustment and development. Nothing was to be recognised as absolute. In his view, there were no absolutes. One's personal view, therefore, became *the* view of the moment.

In whatever way it is presented, at the very roots of postmodern thinking is a fierce independence and an antagonistic atheism. There is no God, so we are free do our own thing, making it up and adjusting it as we go along.

---

[2] R. Wicks, *Friedrich Nietzsche* (an article in the Stanford Encyclopaedia of Philosophy, Mar 15, 2010), retrieved from http://plato.stanford.edu/entries/neitzsche/, p.14
[3] D.J. Bosch, *Transforming Mission-Paradigm shifts in Theology of Mission,* (Orbis, 2008), p.424

In such a worldview, we feel our own way through life, moment by moment, experience by experience, with no set reference points. Robin Usher and Richard Edwards in their book, *Postmodernism and Education: Different Voices, Different World*, stated that, 'Postmodernity, then, describes a world where people have to make their way without fixed referents and traditional anchoring points. It is a world of rapid change, of bewildering instability, where knowledge is constantly changing and meaning "floats."'[4]

Regarding the subject of this book, in postmodern times, the reading and understanding of the Scriptures has often become a matter of personal interpretation, debate and response. It has become known as the 'reader-response' paradigm. This is where one's own personal paradigms and viewpoints become the judge and jury of whether the text is true or not. The truth, therefore, becomes *how I personally see it*.

In my experience as a pastor, this has been used to rationalise a lot of unbiblical behaviour. On occasions, I have asked people about certain moral decisions they've made, and the answer has invariably been, 'Well, it seems good to me. I am personally okay with it.' When asked what God thought about their decision, there was usually a silent and slightly embarrassed shrug.

The concepts of fixed absolutes and eternal truths also make some people nervous to the point of seeking to 'bend' or 'adjust' the truth to make it fit their own circumstances, preferences and lifestyles.

---

[4] R. Usher, and R. Edwards, R., *Postmodernism and Education: Different Voices, Different Worlds*, (New York, Routledge, 1994), p.23

The big issue seems to be over the receptivity of text, and especially the biblical text. Are the Scriptures merely a collection of the thoughts of men, open to as many interpretations as there are individuals, or is there one true, authentic living voice to be heard in them? Does God have a voice? Does He have a view on things? I believe He does.

The Hebrew name for the Bible is *miqra*, meaning 'something to be read.' It is rooted in the word *qara*, which means 'to call out to meet.' In much the same way, the Bible calls out to us, to gather and hear the words of God. This is not just a volume of spiritual data to be collected, analysed and stored; this is a book which, when opened with the right attitude, beckons us to listen for God's voice. Emanating from the Scriptures is the eternal and authoritative voice of God, calling for and insisting on, the attentiveness, the belief and the obedient response of the reader.

Notice I wrote the 'eternal' voice of God. The words of God do not have a shelf life. The Bible itself records that, '*Forever*, O LORD, your word is firmly fixed in the heavens' (Psalm 119:89), 'Long have I known from your testimonies that you have founded them *forever* (Psalm 119:152), and again, 'The sum of your word is truth, and every one of your righteous rules *endures forever*' (Psalm 119:160; all emphases mine).

The Bible is not subject to updates or modifications. As our cultures and philosophies develop, however, there is an increasingly sinister call for the Bible to keep up to date with 'real life.' I would suggest that, on the contrary, we need to keep bringing our ever-changing cultural thinking and values to the eternal thinking and values of Scripture. I particularly like the comment made by Dr Martyn Lloyd-Jones as he spoke of the great doctrines of the atonement and predestination. He said, 'How on earth can you talk of bringing these eternal truths up to date? They are not only up to date, they are and will be ahead of the times to all eternity.'[5]

To deal with the issue of the trustworthiness of the Bible, we will study four areas – the authority, inspiration, inerrancy and infallibility of Scripture.

The Trustworthiness of the Bible

1. Authority: The Bible is *God's Word*. For thousands of years, both Hebrews and Christians have believed that the Old Testament Scriptures are God's Word to all humankind. It contains what He has to say on the issues of life. Moreover, for centuries Christian theologians have believed that the Bible – the entire canon of Scripture – is the final authority on all matters of faith and practice.

The word 'authority' is not a favourite word today, and so it does need to be understood. The main argument for the authority of the Bible is that it contains the words, thoughts, purposes and values of God Himself, and therefore, to dismiss them, or disobey them, is to dismiss and disobey God Himself. The Scriptures contain His voice, and therefore they should command our respect, our attention and most of all, our obedience. It is hugely significant that the two English words 'hear' and 'obey' are just one Hebrew word, *shâma*. The inference is crystal clear: if we do not obey, we have not heard.

---

[5] Dr Martyn Lloyd Jones, cited by Iain H. Murray, *D. Martyn Lloyd-Jones – the First Forty Years*, (Banner of Truth, Edinburgh, 1982), p.71

If we are confused or unsure about what to believe in any given situation, the Scriptures give clear guidance from God's point of view. 'Your word is a lamp to my feet and a light to my path' (Psalm 119:105). If we find elements of God's Word confusing, we are encouraged to ask God for wisdom. James, the half-brother of Jesus, wrote, 'If any of you lacks wisdom, let him ask God, who gives generously to all without reproach, and it will be given him.' (James 1:5).

It is important, then, that we read the Bible with a correct understanding of its authority. If the Bible is not recognised as the final word in all matters of faith and practice, we will be completely at sea. If its authenticity and authority are questioned or doubted, then our spiritual foundations become shaky. If we are not confident about this Bible, then upon what do we stake our life and our future with Christ?

When we take Scripture lightly, we are at the mercy of our own tendencies and perceptions. This 'take it or leave it' attitude is so detrimental to our spiritual growth and can lead us up many a garden path!

Putting it another way: When we make ourselves the judge of the validity and authority of the Scriptures, we put our own views and perceptions above God's. We choose whether or not it carries weight in our lives. Whenever that happens, our respect for God and what He says, will fly out of the window, and our trust in Him and what He says will slowly die. By contrast, when we trust the Bible, we feel its power. How we view this issue, therefore, determines the shape of our theology *and* the depth of our faith.

Why do we need authority? Because we cannot properly govern ourselves. According to the biblical record, humankind was given authority to rule and nurture creation, but sin made destructive inroads into that responsibility. Within a short time, the picture drastically changed, and over thousands of years, we have seen that with no authority, humankind destroys itself. Incidentally, the word 'anarchy' is taken from the Greek word *archē* and means 'without rule'. The biblical picture of anarchy is clearly seen in the book of Judges where we read: 'In those days there was no king in Israel... Everyone did what was right *in his own eyes*' (Judges 17:6; 21:25; emphasis mine). The stories presented in that book show just how evil things became.

God's Word, however, is clear on this (all emphases mine): 'You shall not do according to all that we are doing here today, everyone doing *whatever is right in his own eyes*' (Deuteronomy 12:8); 'The way of a fool is right *in his own eyes*' (Proverbs 12:15); 'All the ways of a man are pure *in his own eyes*' (Proverbs 16:2); 'Every way of a man is right *in his own eyes*' (Proverbs 21:2).

When we trust what *we* see, what *we* feel and what *we* think, then we are barking up the wrong tree. True faith operates, not in the realm of the seen and understood, but in the realm of that which is revealed by the Spirit – the Spirit of Truth.

Even human nature recognises the need for a higher authority. Sin, however, has distorted and severely damaged our human faculties for discernment and apprehension of truth. Our thought processes, emotions and ability to make right choices are all so damaged that they lead us astray. Even our personal conscience, that basic God-given faculty within to help us discern right from wrong, has been conditioned or seared by how we were raised, what we were taught and indwelling sin. It therefore needs re-educating, re-shaping and sharpening by an authority outside itself. And that is exactly what the Bible, in the hands of the Holy Spirit, will do.

There must be a final authority somewhere, some final place to appeal to, some rock upon which we can safely build. Looking to our own powers of reasoning or logic as sources of authority, we elevate them to a place above the God we profess.

The International Standard Bible Encyclopaedia states that 'men need to know what is true, that they may do that which is right. They need some test or standard or court of appeal which distinguishes and enforces the truth; forbids the wrong and commands the right.'[6]

To summarise: Where there is a questioning of the authority of Scripture, the 'every man doing what is right in his own eyes' attitude resurfaces. Questioning the authority of the Bible opens the door for the elevation of our human reasoning above the mind of God. When that happens, everything becomes relative to our own varied understandings of the world, God and even of ourselves. *The* truth becomes *my* truth, as I personally see and understand it. God's Word, however, must stand head and shoulders above our own perceptions.

God, speaking through the prophet Isaiah, said, 'For my thoughts are not your thoughts, neither are your ways my ways, declares the LORD. For as the heavens are higher than the

---

[6] *The International Standard Bible Encyclopaedia*, Article on universal need of authority, e-sword.net

earth, so are my ways higher than your ways and my thoughts than your thoughts' (Isaiah 55:8,9).

Let me conclude this section with a word from Donald Bloesch (1928–2010), an outstanding Evangelical theologian. He wrote, 'Scripture has primacy over other writings; primacy over church tradition; primacy over individual religious experience; primacy over the individual conscience; primacy over individual revelations, dreams and visions; primacy over culture.'[7]

2. Inspiration: The Bible is *heaven-sent*. Many years ago, a man called John Wimber was managing the famous singing band, 'The Righteous Brothers.' He found faith in Christ, and when told he needed to get hold of a Bible – the Word of God – he exclaimed in total surprise, 'What! God wrote a book?'

Well, yes, He did, but He used ordinary human beings to do it. God prepared and inspired men of vastly different backgrounds and temperaments, but they were the secondary authors. God was the Primary Author. The prophet Samuel wrote of the last words of David saying, 'The oracle of David, the son of Jesse, the oracle of a man who was raised on high, the anointed of the God of Jacob, the sweet psalmist of Israel: 'The Spirit of the LORD speaks by me; his word is on my tongue' (2 Samuel 23:1,2).

Jesus, disputing with the religious rulers, made note that King David wrote under the inspiration of the Spirit (see Matthew 22:43). The early apostles believed the same. In their

---

[7] Donald C. Bloesch, cited by Richard Foster, *Streams of Living Water*, (HarperCollins, New York, 1998), p.222

prayer they said, '*Sovereign Lord*, who made the heaven and the earth and the sea and everything in them, *who through the mouth of our father David*, your servant, *said by the Holy Spirit*, 'Why did the Gentiles rage, and the peoples plot in vain?' (Acts 4:25; emphasis mine).

We come back again to Paul's statement to Timothy: 'All Scripture is *breathed out by God* and profitable for teaching, for reproof, for correction, and for training in righteousness, that the man of God may be competent, equipped for every good work' (2 Timothy 3:16; emphasis mine). The Greek word *theopneustos* means literally: 'God-breathed'. Just as God made the heavens and the earth 'by the breath of his mouth' (Psalm 33:6), so it was with the Scriptures. The breath of God resulted in life-generating words of God. For me personally, when I open the pages of my Bible, I sense in my spirit the breath of God.

3. Inerrancy: The Bible is *true*. The internal witness is clear. 'The words of the LORD are pure words, like silver refined in a furnace on the ground, purified seven times' (Psalm 12:6); 'The sum of your word is truth' (Psalm 119:160); 'Sanctify them in the truth; your word is truth' (John 17:17).

You will not find the word 'inerrancy' in the Bible, but like the terms 'Trinity' and 'Incarnation', to name a couple, they are words that describe truths that are nevertheless clearly taught in Scripture. The crucial doctrine of inerrancy teaches that the Bible is completely true, without error.

God does not, and indeed cannot, lie. Neither will He mislead us. It is not in His nature. Deception and lies are, however, in the very nature of Satan. Jesus, speaking of him, said

'He was a murderer from the beginning, and does not stand in the truth, because there is no truth in him. When he lies, he speaks out of his own character, for he is a liar and the father of lies' (John 8:44). Lies and deception do not build trust; they destroy it. God, on the other hand, wants to encourage and build trust into our hearts, and therefore, He will not lie to us.

Klein, Blomberg and Hubbard wrote in their superb book, *Introduction to Biblical Interpretation*, 'for us, the Bible is true in all it intends to teach. Its statements convey what is factual; its record is faithful and reliable.'[8]

This needs to be qualified a little. The various versions of the Bible we read are not inerrant. They are merely translations – some good, some not so good. It is only the *original manuscripts* – the 'autographs' – that can lay claim to being inerrant. But we do not have any of them. Having said that, the thousands of manuscripts we do have, have so few variables in them that they can be counted as being reliable.

I have two more thoughts here: Firstly, it must be said that the more time goes on, the more the Bible is being shown to be correct. For over half a century, I have been systematically reading the Bible, and whenever I look at world events and the state of humanity, I have even more reasons to believe what I see in Scripture. Secondly, there are many who would love to find errors in the Bible. In my experience, however, that attitude has arisen out of a decision to find fault with the Bible in order to rationalise an unbiblical stance.

---

[8] Klein, Blomberg, Hubbard, *Introduction to Biblical Interpretation*, (Word Publishing, Dallas, 1993), p.90

This is nothing new. The apostle Paul wrote to the church in Corinth saying, 'We refuse to practice cunning or *to tamper with God's word...*' (2 Corinthians 4:2; emphasis mine). The apostle Peter, speaking of the writings of Paul, wrote, 'There are some things in them that are hard to understand, which the ignorant and unstable *twist to their own destruction, as they do the other Scriptures*' (2 Peter 3:16; emphasis mine). The word 'twist' is the translation of the Greek word *strebloō*, which means 'to wrench, as if on a rack of torture.'

Jesus Himself said, 'Do not think that I have come to abolish the Law or the Prophets; I have not come to abolish them but to fulfil them. For truly, I say to you, until heaven and earth pass away, *not an iota, not a dot*, will pass from the Law until all is accomplished' (Matthew 5:17,18; emphasis mine). In other words, Jesus believed all the Old Testament writings, saying they would all be fulfilled in Him. He added, 'Therefore whoever *relaxes one of the least* of these commandments and teaches others to do the same, will be called least in the kingdom of heaven, but whoever does them and teaches them will be called great in the kingdom of heaven' (Matthew 5:19; emphasis mine).

4. Infallibility: The Bible is *trustworthy*. Jim Packer said, 'Infallibility signifies the full trustworthiness of a guide that is not deceived and does not deceive.'[9] The Bible can be trusted in all matters of life.

---

[9] J.I. Packer, *Infallibility and Inerrancy*, New Dictionary of Theology, (IVP, Leicester, 1988), p.337

For thousands of years, there have been countless numbers of people who have built their lives upon the words of the Bible, exercising a deep trust and faith in what they found within its pages. They have been the fruitful ones in the earth.

Conclusions

I have sought to demonstrate that the Bible is in fact the Word of God. Although what we have today are English translations of the Hebrew and Greek copies, they are, in the main, remarkably accurate to the original. We can lean on this book for all matters concerning faith and conduct. If we have faith in this Word, we will hear the voice of God, and sense His power working in our lives. If we do not believe and trust this Word, we will receive nothing but dead information.

As we read the Bible, I believe we will begin to hear the Spirit speaking into our hearts. This book is totally unlike any other book. With this book, we learn to listen to a voice. Wayne Grudem wrote:

> Our ultimate conviction that the words of the Bible are God's words comes only when the Holy Spirit speaks in and through the words of the Bible to our hearts and gives us an assurance that these are the words of our Creator speaking to us.[10]

So, let us remind ourselves again of these Scriptures:
'For the word of God is living and active, sharper than any two-edged sword, piercing to the division of soul and of spirit,

---

[10] Wayne Grudem, *Systematic Theology*, (IVP, Leicester, 1994), pp.77,78

of joints and of marrow, and discerning the thoughts and intentions of the heart' (Hebrews 4:12).

'And we also thank God constantly for this, that when you received the word of God, which you heard from us, you accepted it not as the word of men but as what it really is, the word of God, which is at work in you believers' (1 Thessalonians 3:13). The Expanded Translation of this verse ends: '...you welcomed it, not as a word finding its source in men but as it truly is, God's word which is being constantly set in operation in you who believe.'

Hear Eugene Peterson's paraphrase of 2 Timothy 3:16,17 in *The Message*: 'Every part of Scripture is God-breathed and useful one way or another – showing us truth, exposing our rebellion, correcting our mistakes, training us to live God's way. Through the Word we are put together and shaped up for the tasks God has for us.'

The way we approach the Scriptures is of vital importance. It is not merely a textbook containing history, poetry, and spiritual injunctions. Neither is it a compendium of statements that need cutting apart under a technical microscope.

Imagine a beautifully coloured frog moving slowly in a dish. You gaze at it, full of admiration and wonder. Then you take a scalpel and dissect it, exposing all its inner workings. You may have new information, but the frog has lost its beauty; the frog is dead.

I owe a great deal to the writings of Michael Casey, the abbot of a Cistercian monastery in Australia. For my birthday one year, I was given his powerful book *Sacred Reading – the ancient art of Lectio Divina*. As I read it, some of my deeply held convictions were reinforced and expanded. I felt that, in my walking in the world of the Scriptures, I had turned a corner and new vistas opened before me. The joy was unbelievable. In my view, Casey is one of those spiritual masters we all need to listen to if we are going to be serious about our spiritual walk. This book, *Sacred Reading*,[11] is a must for anyone wanting to take read the Bible seriously. Casey taught that it is imperative to come to the Bible with a humble faith and a teachable heart.

The Personal Battles of Two Giants in the Faith

Dr Martyn Lloyd-Jones

Dr Martyn Lloyd-Jones (1899–1981) was one of the greatest expositional preachers of the 20th century. For nearly 30 years he was the minister of Westminster Chapel in London. His preaching ministry and his writings have touched multitudes of people all over the world. He wrote:

> There can be no doubt whatsoever that all the troubles in the Church today, and most of the troubles in the world, are due to a departure from the authority of the Bible. And, alas, it was the Church herself that led in the so-called Higher Criticism that came from Germany just over a hundred years ago. Human philosophy took the place of revelation, man's opinions were exalted and Church leaders talked about 'the advance of knowledge and science', and 'the assured results' of such knowledge. The Bible then became a book just like any other book, out-of-date in certain respects,

---

[11] Michael Casey OSCO, *Sacred Reading*, (Liguori/Triumph, Missouri, 1996), p.6

wrong in other respects, and so on. It was no longer a book on which you could rely implicitly.

There is no question at all that the falling away, even in Church attendance, in this country is the direct consequence of the Higher Criticism. The man in the street says, 'What do these Christians know? It is only their opinion, they are just perpetrating something that the real thinkers and scientists have long since seen through and have stopped considering'. Such is the attitude of the man in the street! He does not listen any longer, he has lost all interest. The whole situation is one of drift; and very largely, I say, it is the direct and immediate outcome of the doubt that has been cast by the Church herself upon her only real authority. Men's opinions have taken the place of God's truth, and the people in their need are turning to the cults, and are listening to any false authority that offers itself to them.

We all therefore have to face this ultimate and final question: Do we accept the Bible as the Word of God, as the sole authority in all matters of faith and practice, or do we not? Is the whole of my thinking governed by Scripture, or do I come with my reason and pick and choose out of Scripture and sit in judgment upon it, putting myself and modern knowledge forward as the ultimate standard and authority? The issue is crystal clear. Do I accept Scripture as a revelation from God, or do I trust to speculation, human knowledge, human learning, human understanding and human reasons, or, putting it still more simply, do I pin my faith to, and subject all my thinking to, what I read in the Bible? Or do I defer to modern knowledge, to modern learning, to what people think today, to what we know at this present time which was not known in the past? It is inevitable that we occupy one or the other of those two positions.[12]

Dr Billy Graham

Dr Billy Graham (1918–2018) was a world-famous evangelist, holding massive crusades in many parts of the world. Through his preaching of the gospel, millions of people found Christ. While he was at Wheaton College in his formative years, he experienced a struggle of faith over the authenticity of the Bible.

He knew that Jesus loved and believed the Old Testament Scriptures, often referring to them. At this point in his life, he was committed to speaking at events as an evangelist and was seeing wonderful results. Yet, in private, he struggled, wondering whether his preaching was based on truth. Billy didn't have an academic mind and he was struggling to find an answer to a lot of the intellectual, scientific and philosophical questions about the veracity of the Bible that some of his tutors were raising.

One night, whilst out for a walk, he came to the point of realising that if he couldn't trust the authenticity of the Bible, he should make the decision, there and then, to give up preaching altogether and go into farming. What happened?

---

[12] Dr Martyn Lloyd-Jones, *The Christian Soldier*, (Banner of Truth, Edinburgh, 1977), pp.210, 211

He dropped to his knees and began to pray. He told God that although there were many things in the Bible that he didn't understand, he was going to trust it. He told the Lord three further things. The first was that he was going to allow faith to override and supersede his doubts and questionings. Secondly, he was going to believe and trust the veracity of the words of the Bible, allowing them to build and shape his life. Thirdly, he was going to preach the Bible's message with all his heart.

As he rose from kneeling in the woods, he knew that a major battle had been fought and won, and a bridge had been crossed in his life. Before the face of God, he had made a deep choice to trust the Bible. In that moment, Billy sensed a fresh awareness of the power and presence of God. From that day, Billy Graham preached the gospel from the Bible, often saying with deep assurance, 'The Bible says...'

The fruit of that decision, during the following six decades of his ministry, was over three million people coming to Christ.

Chapter 3

The Big Story in the Old Testament

I have called this chapter the 'Big Story' for the simple reason that I believe it's so important to read the whole Bible over and over again. That is how we get 'the big story' or, if you prefer, 'the big picture.' As we do this, we find ourselves constructing a framework into which we can place all the various details of the biblical narrative.

I also think it is important to grasp the historical settings of the major events of the Bible. For example, an understanding of who the Assyrians, Persians and Romans were will help put what happened to Israel into context. As we work our way through the big story, world events change; there are huge movements and shifts of world powers. Kingdoms rise and fall. For this reason, I have included some of the major historical events and key players. An important rule of thumb when it comes to understanding the Bible is that context is everything.

Those who take the Bible seriously will find themselves living between two worlds: the ancient world in which the Scriptures were written, and the modern world in which we live. Too often we look at the ancient world of the Bible through our modern mindsets, and in doing so, we miss important things. It is essential that we read not only the texts of the Bible, but we learn about the historical background and cultural influences during the times of the writers.

I have often come across believers who have selections of favourite passages that they read repeatedly. The difficulty with this method is that these Scriptures are often seen out of context and can become disjointed. I will explain this in more detail later in the book.

This chapter began its life as a question put to a young man who was being interviewed for the role of the Director of *Youth for Christ* in Lincoln. I was on the interviewing panel, and I asked him to give me a summary of the whole message of the Bible in five minutes. I felt it was important that whoever got the job had a good handle on what the Bible was all about! He took a deep breath and then delivered his thoughts in the said time. He did well, I might add, and he got his own back when he interviewed me, some years later, at a youth event!

Afterwards, I was asked by the leadership of our church to present the whole story of the Bible to a Sunday school class in 15 minutes. It was a challenge, but I managed to do it and furthermore they understood it! Sometime later, I presented a longer version to the church with a PowerPoint, taking the customary 45 minutes. I called it 'The Big Story'. It then became a lecture in a series of lectures upon which this book is based. I have since done further research and have enlarged it. So, here goes.

The Beginning of Things

The book of Genesis contains the beginning of many things. In the first 11 chapters, we see the creation of the heavens and the earth, the creation of humankind, the origin of sin, and the beginning of the nations.

When people talk of the creation of the heavens and the earth, questions are raised – was it creation or was it evolution? Was it created in seven days or seven periods of time?

Archbishop James Ussher (1581–1656) has been called one of the finest scholars of his day in the Christian church. He was famous for his chronological work on the dating of creation, using biblical data from Adam right through to Moses. Using the universally accepted date for the commencement of the building of Solomon's temple (967 BC), he worked back to the date of the Exodus (1547 BC), then back to Adam and Eve, arriving at 4004 BC for the creation of Adam. He felt that the seven days of creation were literal and therefore deduced that the earth was created at the same time. His monumental work, *Annals of the Old Testament, deduced from the First Origins of the World*, contained over 12,000 footnotes from secular sources and another 2,000 references from the Bible and the Apocrypha. I have crunched the numbers myself and have come up with the slightly different date of 4027 BC.

Of course, in the light of scientific knowledge, much of this has been brought into question. Charles Darwin introduced the world to the theory of evolution, and it became the sandy bedrock for many (pun intended)! Since then, many debates have taken place between Christian evolutionists and Christian creationists. The debates still go on between great minds in both camps. There are books and articles galore, and you can read them for yourself.

For me, the question is not so much *how* God created the heavens and the earth, or *how long* He took to do it, but *the fact that* He did it. The Bible says, 'By faith we understand that the universe was created by the word of God, so that what is seen was not made out of things that are visible' (Hebrews 11:3). If this is true, and I believe it is, then, very simply, Genesis must be understood from a supernatural point of view.

The Creation of Adam and Eve

After the spectacular creations of the heavens and the earth, the wildlife and vegetation, God created His masterpiece. Before the appearance of Adam and Eve, two unique individuals made in the image of God, God was simply building the stage. Of all creation, the man and the woman were specifically created with the potential to have a relationship with God.

I want to spend some time here because, in these few chapters, theological seeds are sown. Much of what Christians believe has its origin in this remarkable book of Genesis. Indeed, this may be a chief reason why liberal theologians and natural thinkers have so severely attacked this book. The *ESV Study Bible*, in its introduction to this book, contains these words: 'The English title 'Genesis' comes from the Greek translation of the Pentateuch and means 'origin', a very apt title because Genesis is all about origins – of the world, of the human race, of sin, and of the Jewish people. The Hebrew title

[*Bereshith*] is translated 'in the Beginning' using the first phrase of the book.'[1]

The first thing we notice about Adam is **his constitution** – he was 'made in the image of God, according to His likeness' (Genesis 1:26,27). This refers not to his physiology, but to the makeup of his soul. He had the capacity to think, to feel emotions and to make choices. Like his creator, he could be creative. Out of all created beings, only human beings are given the status of being made in God's image, and this gives them a certain specialness.[2]

In the second chapter of Genesis we read, 'then the LORD God formed the man of dust from the ground and breathed into his nostrils the breath of life, and the man became a living creature' (Genesis 2:7). As the breath of God entered him, the man started to breathe on his own. More literally, the man became 'a living breather.' Job said, 'The Spirit of God has made me, and the breath of the Almighty gives me life' (Job 33:4).

The oft used expression, 'took their last breath', is an accurate picture of death. Job also said, 'If he should set his heart to it and gather to himself his spirit and his breath, all flesh would perish together, and man would return to dust' (Job 34:14). *The Message* puts it quite bluntly: 'If he decided to hold his breath, every man, woman, and child would die for lack of air.' On the Cross, Jesus 'uttered a loud cry and breathed his last' (Mark 15:37-39 / Luke 23:46 / Acts 5,10; 12:53).

Physically, however, Adam was made from the dust, and upon his death, to dust he would return (Genesis 2:7; 3:19). The

---

[1] T. D. Alexander, *Introduction to Genesis*, ESV Study Bible, (Crossway Bibles, Illinois, 2008), p.39
[2] See David Atkinson, *The Message of Genesis 1-11*, (IVP, Leicester, 1990), p.40

name Adam is taken from the Hebrew word *adamah* which means 'the ground, the earth.' The book of Job, probably written before Genesis, talks of humans as 'those who dwell in houses of clay, whose foundation is in the dust' (Job 4:19). Job, in his conversation with God says, 'Remember that you have made me like clay; and will you return me to the dust?' (Job 10:9) The prophet Isaiah prayed, 'But now, O LORD, you are our Father; we are the clay, and you are our potter; we are all the work of your hand' (Isaiah 64:8). Maybe that is what the apostle Paul meant when he wrote to the Corinthians 'But we have this treasure in jars of clay, to show that the surpassing power belongs to God and not to us' (2 Corinthians 4:7).

The Latin word for soil or earth is *humus*, and is connected to our word *humility*, possibly to remind us that because we are of the earth, we should keep our feet on the ground. True humility knows, and is content, in its proper place.

The second thing we notice about Adam is **Eve**. In the first chapter of Genesis we read, 'Then God said, "Let us make man in our image, after our likeness. And let them have dominion over the fish of the sea and over the birds of the heavens and over the livestock and over all the earth and over every creeping thing that creeps on the earth." So God created man in his own image, in the image of God he created him; *male and female he created them*' (Genesis 1:26,27; emphasis mine). This is further expounded in the next chapter: 'Then the LORD God said, "It is not good that the man should be alone; I will make him a helper fit for him." ... So the LORD God caused a deep sleep to fall upon the man, and while he slept took one of his ribs and closed up its place with flesh. And the rib that the LORD God had taken from the man he made into a woman and brought her to the man' (Genesis 2:18–22).

Adam was not designed to be a solitary mystic or a freelancer, but one who would live in relationship, not only with his Maker, but also with those God put around him, within a certain pattern and with responsibility. His deepest relationship on the earth was to come. God the Creator noticed Adam's deep loneliness amid an earth teeming with life he couldn't communicate with, and put him into a deep sleep. From his side, God created a woman. Derek Kidner wrote,

> Companionship is presented in Eden as a primary human need, which God proceeded to meet by creating not Adam's duplicate but his opposite and complement, and by uniting the two, male and female, in perfect personal harmony.[3]

The third thing we notice about Adam and Eve is **their calling**. The calling had two dimensions to it, seen from two Scriptures. Firstly, 'Be fruitful and multiply and fill the earth and subdue it, and have dominion over the fish of the sea and over the birds of the heavens and over every living thing that moves on the earth' (Genesis 1:28). Secondly, 'The LORD God took the man and put him in the garden of Eden to work it and keep it' (Genesis 2:15). Their destiny was to become the most prominent of all God's creatures on the earth, populating it with the human species, and wisely leading and directing all things. It was also to 'work (cultivate) and keep (look after)' their immediate environment.

---

[3] Derek Kidner, *Genesis*, (Tyndale Press, London, 1973), pp.35,36

Unfortunately, after the fall (see point four), the cultivation somehow turned into manipulation, and the keeping turned into misusing and abusing. The care and enjoyment of the garden turned into the commercial exploitation of the earth. Watchman Nee, a Chinese pastor imprisoned for the last 20 years of his life for his faith, wrote several powerful and penetrating books. One of them was on the Song of Songs, where he wrote about that first garden in Eden:

> ...after the creation of the universe and man, God planted a garden. A garden is neither common ground nor ground for the planting of things at random, nor is it ground for mere agricultural purposes, but the production of something for beauty and pleasure. In a garden there may be trees; but the thought is not for timber. There may be fruit, but the value is not calculated in terms of commercial produce.[4]

Though set in a garden to nurture and take care of God's creation, humankind degenerated, exploiting and mishandling it all, demonstrating that in our fallen state we are not capable of wisely stewarding the earth and all that lives upon it.

The fourth thing we notice is **their fall**. Somehow, into this garden came a malevolent spirit manifesting itself in the form of a serpent. The Hebrew word used is *nâchâsh* (pronounced naw chawsh) which means a snake. It is derived from the primitive root *nâchash* (pronounced naw chash), meaning properly, 'to hiss, that is, whisper' and 'to practise divination.' As

---

[4] Watchman Nee, *The Song of Songs*, (Christian Literature Crusade, London, 1966), p.107

we read on through the Bible, we clearly begin to see that this was Satan, the adversary of God.

It began with Satan sowing a thought in Eve's mind that cast doubt on what God had said to Adam and an aspersion on the character of God. The unchallenged thought turned into a curious desire and ended with a bad choice. Satan still works this way, sowing evil, negative and perverse thoughts into human minds. In order not to repeat such a mistake ourselves, we need to learn to challenge and take captive the thoughts that knock on the door of our minds (see 2 Corinthians 10:5).

The fifth thing we notice is **their plight**. They became soiled by sin, separated from God and sentenced to death. God had warned Adam with these words, 'And the LORD God commanded the man, saying, "You may surely eat of every tree of the garden, but of the tree of the knowledge of good and evil you shall not eat, for in the day that you eat of it you shall surely die"' (Genesis 2:16,17).

They had eaten of the tree, and now the death sentence was passed. It was firstly to Adam and Eve, and then to all who would come from them. It did not happen immediately ('in the day' refers to the consequence, not the literal time) but eventually. They came from the earth, and to the earth they would return. It became the fate of all created beings. Centuries later, sensing death was near, Joshua used this phrase: 'And now I am about to go the way of all the earth...' (Joshua 23:14). Many years later, King David would use the same words (1 Kings 2:2).

Something else died too. I believe it was the faculties of Adam and Eve's spirits, those inner abilities to perceive and relate to God. From this point, Adam and Eve lost the immediate sense of God, and from there on operated only out of memory. The intimacy was gone.

The chasm between them and God was immediately apparent. They hid themselves from Him, fearing punishment and feeling shame. They tried to cover themselves with fig leaves. Then the blame-shifting erupted. Eve blamed the serpent, and Adam blamed Eve.

The sixth thing we notice is **their restoration**. God came to them, speaking firstly to the serpent, ending with the prophetic words, 'I will put enmity between you and the woman, and between your offspring and her offspring; he shall bruise your head, and you shall bruise his heel' (Genesis 3:15). This statement is called the *protevangelium* – the first gospel proclamation. One born of a woman would crush the serpent.

God turns to the hapless pair and brings His judgments concerning childbirth and the cursing of the earth, ending with the words, 'for you are dust, and to dust you shall return' (Genesis 3:19). This sentence has not been rescinded. The death of Christ on the Cross, removed the sting, not the event.

Then God did something remarkable. He uncovered them and He covered them. Their own fig leaf attempts to hide their nakedness were futile, and certainly would not have lasted. So, 'The LORD God made for Adam and for his wife garments of skins and clothed them' (Genesis 3:21). The question arises – where did the skins come from? In my view, a creature (maybe a lamb) lost its life to cover the guilty ones, and thereby a long-lasting principle was set in place: an innocent one dies for the guilty one, and the sin is covered.

The consequences of sin soon spilt into the world, wreaking untold devastation. In Genesis 4, the first murder occurs. Cain, Adam and Eve's firstborn, murdered his younger brother over an issue of worship. Cain brought an offering from the fields and Abel brought a lamb. God rejected Cain's offering because it was the work of his own hands and recognised and accepted Abel's because Abel had understood the principle that had been set – the innocent dies for the guilty, and the sin is covered. If we understand this principle, we will gain an understanding of the Cross of Christ and the Lamb of God who was slain for the sin of the world.

In these chapters we have some remarkable incidents of longevity. The oldest man in the Bible was Methuselah. Some translators feel that his name means 'man of the dart or javelin,' but it can equally mean 'When he dies, judgment' or 'When he is dead, it shall be sent' or 'he dies; a sending forth'. This was one of God's long-term prophecies. Imagine carrying that for 969 years! What a conversation stopper! In fact, a study of the biblical chronology will reveal that the year of his death was the year of the global Flood, giving a date of 2359 BC.

The Flood was God's judgment on the earth. He instructed Noah to build an ark – a large boat that would house his immediate family and a selection of the animal world. Taking the biblical cubit as 18 inches, this boat was 450ft long, 75ft wide and 45ft high. It would have a displacement of 40–50 thousand tons. Just for a comparison, HMS Victory was 227ft long and 52ft wide, just half the length of Noah's ark!

After the global Flood, which decimated everything living on the earth, except those in the ark, the mandate to repopulate the earth is re-given to Noah and his sons and daughters. God said, 'Be fruitful and multiply and fill the earth' (Genesis 9:1). The deep tragedy is that sin was not eradicated by the flood. Being a descendant of Adam and Eve, the sickness lived on in Noah and his descendants.

From this point, we see the beginnings of the three major people groups. It is written, 'The sons of Noah who went forth from the ark were Shem, Ham, and Japheth. (Ham was the father of Canaan.) These three were the sons of Noah, and from these the people of the whole earth were dispersed' (Genesis 9:18,19). The three families are scattered in three directions, becoming the progenitors of the three major people groups. The tenth chapter of Genesis gives us a comprehensive picture of the expansion of the families into 70 various nations of the known earth. According to the *ESV Study Bible*, 'In general, the descendants of Ham settled in North Africa and the Eastern Mediterranean coast, the descendants of Shem in Mesopotamia and Arabia, and the descendants of Japheth in Europe and the greater area of Asia Minor.'[5]

As the story further unfolds, we see the comment that 'the earth had one language and the same words' (Genesis 11:1). That was about to change, however. Some years later in the land of Shinar (Ancient Babylonia), humankind had a desire to establish a name for themselves and prevent their dispersion throughout the earth. So, they decided to build a city and a tower. God thwarted their plans and confused their languages. David Atkinson makes this comment:

---

[5] T. D. Alexander, *Introduction to Genesis*, ESV Study Bible, (Crossway Bibles, Illinois, 2008), p.67

The story of the tower of Babel is a sad description of the fracture of community, of a breakdown of fellowship, of a failure in communication, of a growth in isolation and confusion. It all results from a communal failure to live in dependence upon God, and insistence on striving to reach the heavens, and from giving way instead to pride in human achievements and power, and from human beings' determination to be the source of their own security. Does that carry a social warning which the world, then and now, needs to hear?[6]

The Birth of a Nation

The virus of sin was still on the ascendant, but then came another turning point in the big story. Up to this point, the narrative has been concerned with the big picture of the creation of the earth and the heavens, Adam and Eve, the Fall, the Flood, followed by the history of humankind as a whole. Now, the story centres again on one man – Abram, one of Shem's descendants. These were Shemites or, as they are more widely known, Semites.

At the time, Abram was living in a large city called Ur, in Babylonia (Modern Tell el-Muqayyar in Iraq – 186 miles southeast of Baghdad). Around 250,000 people lived there, and the city was dominated by a temple dedicated to the worship of Nannar, sometimes called Sin, the moon god. By now, the monotheism (belief in one God) of the first 11 chapters had disappeared into a saturation of polytheism (belief in many gods). It is estimated that by this time, there were hundreds of

---
[6] David Atkinson, *The Message of Genesis 1-11*, (IVP, Leicester, 1990), p.177

gods and demi-gods which were personifications of the elements and perceived powers in the world.[7]

There is no record of the details, but suddenly God revealed Himself to Abram, and said to him, 'Go from your country and your kindred and your father's house to the land that I will show you. And I will make of you a great nation, and I will bless you and make your name great, so that you will be a blessing' (Genesis 12:1,2).

From Abram, God was going to create a new nation. None of the nations mentioned above fitted the bill. There was a command to leave everything, and then there was a two-fold promise of firstly, a new homeland and, secondly, an immense new family. The writer to the Hebrews puts it this way: 'By faith Abraham [Abram] obeyed when he was called to go out to a place that he was to receive as an inheritance. And he went out, not knowing where he was going' (Hebrews 11:8). He left by faith and journeyed by faith, albeit by a very circuitous route, and it was only when he got there that God said to him, 'To your offspring I will give this land' (Genesis 12:7).

There was another issue. Sarai, Abram's wife, was unable to have children. So, to facilitate the promise of a son (Genesis 15:4), Sarai gave her Egyptian slave girl to Abram. This was socially acceptable in their culture, but it flew in the face of God's plans. Sarai's plan 'was one more example of the futility of human efforts to achieve God's blessings.'[8] Hagar, the Egyptian slave girl, was mistreated by the progenitors of Israel.

---

[7] See G. E. Wright, *An Introduction to Biblical Archaeology*, (Duckworth, London, 1960), p.1
[8] J.H. Sailhamer, *Genesis, NIV Bible Commentary*, (Hodder & Stoughton, London, 1994), p.25

It is ironic that in centuries to come, Israel would be mistreated by Egypt. The ultimate results of Sarai's action were friction, rejection, hatred and the beginnings of an animosity that is still felt today.

We get a similar scenario a few chapters later, where it is written, 'thus both the daughters of Lot [Abram's nephew] became pregnant by their father. The firstborn bore a son and called his name Moab. He is the father of the Moabites to this day. The younger also bore a son and called his name Ben-ammi. He is the father of the Ammonites to this day' (Genesis 19:36–38). Both these boys became the fathers of nations who would eventually become vicious enemies of God's people.

It is also interesting to note that several barren women in the Bible gave birth, by answer to prayer and supernatural means, to significant children. Sarai gave birth to Isaac (Genesis 21:1,2); Rebekah gave birth to Jacob and Esau (Genesis 25:21–26); Rachel gave birth to Joseph (Genesis 30:22–24); Manoah's wife gave birth to Samson (Judges 13:24); Hannah gave birth to Samuel (1 Samuel 1:20); Elizabeth gave birth to John the Baptist (Luke 1:57).

God spoke again to Abram, changing his name to Abraham. The 'exalted father' was changed to 'father of a multitude.' The promise of a son is then reiterated with more detail. God went on to say, 'As for Sarai your wife, you shall not call her name Sarai, but Sarah shall be her name. I will bless her, and moreover, I will give you a son by her. I will bless her, and she shall become nations; kings of peoples shall come from her' (Genesis 17:15–16). Around 20 years after this promise, Sarah gave birth to Isaac.

The story gathers pace. Isaac became the father of Jacob who, like his grandfather and grandmother, had his name changed. Jacob became Israel and went on to become the father of 12 sons. Those sons come from four different mothers. Again, this was very much ancient Near Eastern cultural behaviour, though it caused all sorts of trouble for Jacob! These 12 sons eventually became the 12 tribes of Israel.

At this point, it is important to reflect on something God said to Abram (before he became Abraham) years before Isaac was born. The Lord said to him, 'Know for certain that your offspring will be sojourners in a land that is not theirs and will be servants there, and they will be afflicted for four hundred years. But I will bring judgment on the nation that they serve, and afterward they shall come out with great possessions' (Genesis 15:13,14).

Joseph now enters the story. He was born to Rachel, Jacob's favourite wife, and became Jacob's favourite son. Early in life he began to receive dreams from God about his future, but they were rejected by his brothers. Determined to get rid of him, they sold him as a slave, and he ended up in Egypt. There he was bought by Potiphar, Pharaoh's captain of the guard.

God's hand was upon him, yet he found himself falsely accused by Potiphar's wife and thrown into prison. Even there, the hand of the Lord was upon him, and sometime later, he interpreted the dreams of two of his cellmates. Two years afterwards, this came to the attention of Pharaoh, who himself had been on the receiving end of disturbing dreams. Joseph was quickly brought out of prison to interpret them. With prophetic eyes, he saw seven years of famine coming, and then gave practical advice on how to deal with the situation. Sensing the wisdom of God in him, Pharaoh elevated him to the second highest position in the land. Joseph's early dreams began to be fulfilled.

Famine indeed struck both Egypt and Palestine, and eventually Jacob and the whole family moved to Egypt. Joseph was reconciled to his brothers, and the family survived the famine. The ancient prophecy of Abram started to unfold. Years later, sensing the nearness of his death, Joseph said to his brothers, 'I am about to die, but God will visit you and bring you up out of this land to the land that he swore to Abraham, to Isaac, and to Jacob' (Genesis 50:24). Abram's prophecy was now underlined and confirmed.

Following the death of Joseph, and two Pharaohs later, the descendants of Jacob had multiplied, filling the land of Egypt. Another Pharaoh came to the throne, who knew nothing of the history of Joseph. Fearful of their numerical power, this Pharaoh (believed to be Thutmose III who reigned from 1483 BC to 1450 BC), began to oppress the people first by enslaving them, and then commanding that all future Hebrew male infants should be slain.

Into these troubled times, Moses was born and miraculously preserved from death by Pharaoh's own daughter. Raised as a prince of Egypt, he was taught at the highest levels. Stephen testified before the Sanhedrin that Moses was 'instructed in all the wisdom of the Egyptians, and he was mighty in his words and deeds' (Acts 7:22).

The Big Rescue

At the age of 40, Moses entered a major identity crisis. He had been born a Hebrew, but raised as an Egyptian prince, and the time came 'when Moses had grown up, he went out to his people and looked on their burdens, and he saw an Egyptian beating a Hebrew, one of his people. He looked this way and that, and seeing no one, he struck down the Egyptian and hid him in the sand' (Exodus 2:11,12).

Two Scriptures are significant at this point. The first is found again in Stephen's speech: 'He supposed that his brothers would understand that God was giving them salvation by his hand, but they did not understand' (Acts 7:24). The second is found in the letter to the Hebrews: 'By faith Moses, when he was grown up, refused to be called the son of Pharaoh's daughter, choosing rather to be mistreated with the people of God than to enjoy the fleeting pleasures of sin. He considered the reproach of Christ greater wealth than the treasures of Egypt, for he was looking to the reward' (Hebrews 11:24–26). In the depths of his heart, Moses knew that he was a Hebrew, and in that inner conflict, his deepest roots won.

After fleeing Egypt, he spent another 40 years in the wilderness, got married, and looked after the flock of Jethro, his father-in-law. The prince had become a shepherd – all part of the divine training.

At the age of 80, Moses had a powerful encounter with God (the burning bush story – Exodus 3), who commanded him to return to Egypt to lead the Hebrews out of their slavery. At first Moses faltered, wrestling with a deep sense of failure and inadequacy. Dr Alan Cole made this insightful observation:

'Moses, unlike his earlier days in Egypt, had learned to distrust himself so thoroughly that he will incur God's anger (Exodus 4:14). Self-distrust is good, but only if it leads to trust in God. Otherwise, it ends as spiritual paralysis, inability and unwillingness to undertake any course of action. Moses, like Elijah (1 Kings 19:3,4), is a picture of a man who had had a nervous breakdown and is now unwilling to work for God at all.'[9]

However, Moses won through this battle and then returned to Egypt with a strong sense of God's hand upon him. He met with firm resistance from the then Pharaoh (believed to be Amenhotep II who reigned from 1450 BC to 1423 BC). Nevertheless, under the leadership of Moses, and through ten powerful miracles that demonstrated the supremacy of God over the principal gods of Egypt, Pharaoh's power was broken. The final miracle was the judgement of God in taking the lives of the first-born children of all the Egyptians. Moreover, God was going to demonstrate salvation by the blood of a lamb. The children of Israel were told to place the blood of a sacrificed lamb over the doorposts and lintels of their houses. This was to prevent the destroying angel from God taking the lives of their first-born children. This event later became the origin of the Jewish Passover - named because the angel of death 'passed over' the houses marked with blood. Centuries later, One would come as the Lamb of God, who by His own blood, would bring salvation to all who believe.

This final miracle shattered Pharaoh and all of Egypt, who then told the Israelites to leave immediately. So they left,

---

[9] Alan Cole, *Tyndale Commentary on Exodus,* (Tyndale Press, London, 1973), p.68

ladened with gifts. Miraculously, they crossed the Red Sea (more correctly, the 'Sea of Reeds'), and entered the wilderness, eventually coming to Sinai, the mountain of God.

The story of the Exodus was of great significance, and it became etched into the life of the nation. However, what followed was the tetchiness of the Hebrews in the wilderness, the dramatic giving of the Ten Commandments, and the construction of the tent of meeting, otherwise known as the 'tabernacle'. The sacred furniture for this tent was also commissioned and built; the ark of the covenant, the altar of incense, the seven-branched candlestick and the table for the bread of the presence. The tabernacle was a holy place where God would meet with His people, and it was specifically designed to travel with them on their journey. Moses also had the difficult task of shaping this recalcitrant group of people into a nation.

Their first encounter with the Promised Land was an unmitigated disaster. Their resolve was demolished by the negative report brought by ten of the 12 spies sent in to survey the land (despite the passionate and godly report of the other two spies – Caleb and Joshua). God's anger broke out and the whole nation was turned back into the wilderness, to wander aimlessly for another 40 years. During this time, under the judgment of God, all the adults perished and were buried in the desert.

One day, in a lecture I was giving on this subject, I saw, in my imagination, hundreds of thousands of people coming out of the desert, and as I looked, none of them were over the age of 60 years, except for two old men well into their eighties. I asked one of them, 'Where are all the grandfathers and grandmothers? Where are all the aged ones?' I received the reply, 'We have buried them all back there in dirt graves in the desert where we have been wandering for the last 40 years. We buried them at an average rate of 40 a day, or 290 a week, or 1250 a month. We have lost over 600,000 people.'

There was further tragedy to come. The people grumbled yet again and, in Numbers 20:2-13, we read how Moses completely lost it with them. He then came under the judgment of God for his violent outburst of frustration and anger.

Walter Kaiser wrote, 'The accumulated anger and frustration of forty years bore down on Moses.'[10] The Psalmist put it this way: 'They angered him at the waters of Meribah, and it went ill with Moses on their account, for they made his spirit bitter, and he spoke rashly with his lips' (Psalm 106:32,33). For this, God told Moses that he would not lead the people into the Promised Land. He would look upon it, but not enter it. Another man would have that responsibility. In Deuteronomy 34:1-8, we have the moving account of his death before the Lord, ending with the poignant 'and God buried him.'

The Big History

Here is an interesting Scripture. God spoke to Moses just as they were poised to enter the Land:

> Speak to the people of Israel and say to them, 'When you pass over the Jordan into the land of Canaan, then

---

[10] Walter Kaiser Jr, *Exodus, NIV Bible Commentary, Vol 1,* (Hodder & Stoughton, London, 1994), p.210

you shall drive out all the inhabitants of the land from before you and destroy all their figured stones and destroy all their metal images and demolish all their high places. And you shall take possession of the land and settle in it, for I have given the land to you to possess it. You shall inherit the land by lot according to your clans. To a large tribe you shall give a large inheritance, and to a small tribe you shall give a small inheritance. Wherever the lot falls for anyone, that shall be his. According to the tribes of your fathers you shall inherit. But if you do not drive out the inhabitants of the land from before you, then those of them whom you let remain shall be as barbs in your eyes and thorns in your sides, and they shall trouble you in the land where you dwell. And I will do to you as I thought to do to them' (Numbers 33:50–56).

At this point, Joshua enters the story as the successor to Moses. His task was to take the people over the Jordan River and conquer the Land, relocating the tribes into their God-given inheritances. Each of the tribes were allocated a different area to subdue and live in. This took place slowly over a long period of time and was not entirely successful. Many pockets of resistance remained.

The failure to totally subdue the land brought about this rebuke from the Angel of the Lord: 'I brought you up from Egypt and brought you into the land that I swore to give to your fathers. I said, "I will never break my covenant with you, and you shall make no covenant with the inhabitants of this land; you shall break down their altars." But you have not obeyed my voice. What is this you have done? So now I say, I will not drive them out before you, but they shall become thorns in your sides, and their gods shall be a snare to you' (Judges 2:1-3).

After the death of Joshua, the Bible says:

> There arose another generation after them who did not know the LORD or the work that he had done for Israel. And the people of Israel did what was evil in the sight of the LORD and served the Baals. And they abandoned the LORD, the God of their fathers, who had brought them out of the land of Egypt. They went after other gods, from among the gods of the peoples who were around them and bowed down to them... So the anger of the LORD was kindled against Israel, and he gave them over to plunderers, who plundered them. And he sold them into the hand of their surrounding enemies, so that they could no longer withstand their enemies (Judges 2:10-14).

The times of the Judges were a period of 'Dark Ages' in the story of the children of Israel. They had entered the Promised Land as a nation, in covenant relationship with God, held together by His Law and His presence. Very quickly, however, they degenerated into tribalism, idolatry and individualism. The key Scripture for this period is 'Everyone did what was right in their own eyes.' This comment is found four times in the book of Judges (17:6; 18:1; 19:1; 21:25).

The first chapter in Judges gives a catalogue of failures in driving out the inhabitants. It was incomplete obedience, and from then on, Israel's behaviour was marked by a repeated cycle of rebellion against the Lord, followed by divinely sanctioned oppression, followed by the nation crying to God for help, followed by God's deliverance by the hand of a prophetic judge, followed by a time of rest for the land, followed by further rebellion against the Lord.

There were 12 judges in all, and one of them was a woman. They were charismatic leaders who were specifically raised up by God to deliver wayward Israel from their various oppressors, but they were by no means perfect. The only one who stands out as an example of not only faith, but virtue, is Deborah.

David Howard wrote,

> All servants of God's purposes for his people have their flaws; the question is whether God should choose to allow those flaws to bear their bitter fruit. Even in these circumstances, God is working out his plan; he is not thwarted, even by human failure.[11]

Eventually the people wanted a king, just like the surrounding nations. The Bible records this: 'Then all the elders of Israel gathered together and came to Samuel at Ramah and said to him, "Behold, you are old and your sons do not walk in your ways. Now appoint for us a king to judge us like all the nations." But the thing displeased Samuel when they said, "Give us a king to judge us." And Samuel prayed to the LORD. And the LORD said to Samuel, "Obey the voice of the people in all that they say to you, for they have not rejected you, but they have rejected me from being king over them"' (1 Samuel 8:4–7).

The next period of Israel's history (971–586 BC) was the reign of the kings. The first monarch was Saul. He had a physically commanding presence. He was incredibly

---

[11] David M. Howard Jr, *Introduction to Judges*, ESV study Bible, p.435

courageous, and powerfully anointed by the Holy Spirit. Inwardly, however, he was not up to the role.

Fleming James writes, 'The Bible brands him as a rejected man. There was in Saul a fatal weakness. With all his zeal for Yahweh [the Lord] he could not be depended upon to obey Yahweh's will. Under pressure he would go his own way rather than the way he himself conceived to be God's. He lacked the power to subordinate the impulse of the moment to the long advantage of the future.'[12] Saul failed time and time again, disobeying God when under pressure from circumstances and the people. In the end, God rejected him, and, after resorting to a spirit medium, he died by suicide in battle. But by then God had sought and found 'a man after his own heart' (1 Samuel 13:14).

This man was David. He was the youngest son of a Bethlehem farmer called Jesse. The Hebrew word *haqqaton* – the youngest – carries undertones of insignificance. He was the family runt.

The story of David and Goliath (found in 1 Samuel 17) is probably the single most narrated story in the whole Bible. We know more about him than any other biblical character. It was under David's rule all the tribes of Israel were united into one nation. We can roughly establish that Saul began to reign from 1051 BC and reigned for 40 years (Acts 13:21). David then, began to reign in 1011 BC, and he also reigned 40 years. He brought the tabernacle into Jerusalem.

David then fell badly, firstly by committing adultery with Bathsheba, and then by having her husband purposely killed in

---

[12] Fleming James, *Personalities of the Old Testament*, (Scribners, 1939), pp.113,114

a battle scenario to cover his tracks. God saw it, however, and brought a stinging rebuke to him through Nathan the prophet. David repented, but there was consequential damage within the family dynamics. Bathsheba's first child died, but her subsequent son by David was Solomon.

Solomon succeeded David in 971 BC, reigning also for 40 years. He was the one who constructed the first temple, replacing the tabernacle. His son, Rehoboam, then took the throne, and during his reign, according to a prophetic word given to Jeroboam, the kingdom was sadly divided.

In 931 BC, Jeroboam established the Northern Kingdom – Israel – with Samaria as its capital city, and Rehoboam held on to the greatly reduced Southern kingdom – Judah – with Jerusalem as its capital. For the next 345 years, a mixture of good and evil kings reigned over the two kingdoms, often waging war against each other.

Right in the middle of all this, four scrolls were written, which became the bedrock of the devotional life of Israel. The Psalms became the song / prayer book of the Hebrew people. Proverbs and Ecclesiastes were wisdom literature, and the Song of Solomon was a love poem between a king and his beloved, foreshadowing the intimate relationship between Christ and His 'bride', the church.

This was also the time of the prophets. These were individuals who drew close to God, hearing His voice, and understanding the divine perspective on the life of the nation. They brought God's voice and viewpoint, and many suffered for it. They consistently preached against the immoralities and idolatries of the two nations, and they warned that God was going to bring judgment. Some also saw glimpses of the coming Messiah.

The Big Captivity

From the time of their separation, the two kingdoms became vulnerable to invasion from greater powers. There were, in fact, several separate occasions when incursions were made, and people were either killed or taken into exile. Here are the main events:

The first was an invasion by the Egyptian king Shishak around 926 BC. He swept through both Judah and Israel, taking 150 cities, and severely looting Jerusalem. Scripture records, 'In the fifth year of King Rehoboam, Shishak king of Egypt came up against Jerusalem. He took away the treasures of the house of the LORD and the treasures of the king's house. He took away everything. He also took away all the shields of gold that Solomon had made' (1 Kings 14:25,26).

The second major invasion was made by Tiglath-Pileser, the king of Assyria, during his military campaigns in 733–732 BC. He captured swathes of towns and cities in the Northern and Eastern regions of Israel, carrying many captives to Assyria. The Bible records, 'In the days of Pekah king of Israel, Tiglath-Pileser king of Assyria came and captured Ijon, Abel-beth-maacah, Janoah, Kedesh, Hazor, Gilead, and Galilee, all the land of Naphtali, and he carried the people captive to Assyria' (2 Kings 15:29).

The third one took place ten years later. In 722 BC, Shalmaneser, the new king of Assyria, came to the Northern kingdom and besieged it for three years. The Bible records, 'In the ninth year of Hoshea, the king of Assyria captured Samaria, and he carried the Israelites away to Assyria and placed them in Halah, and on the Habor, the river of Gozan, and in the cities of the Medes' (2 Kings 17:6). The Northern Kingdom would never exist as its own entity again.

Ten years later, Sennacherib, the next Assyrian king, returned, and conquered some of the fortified cities of Judah (now the Southern Kingdom, ruled from Jerusalem). Emboldened by this, he attempted to take Jerusalem, only to meet with the forces of heaven. A solitary angel of the Lord went out and killed 185,000 men of the Assyrian army. Sennacherib returned to Nineveh (the capital of Assyria) in shame and was subsequently assassinated by his two sons. In the time of his grandson, Ashurbanipal, Assyria expanded to its greatest extent over the known world.

In the decades afterwards, there came seismic movements. There were various skirmishes with Babylonia. Egypt rebelled and began to assert itself. Assyria gradually went into decline and was driven out of Babylonia in 625 BC. In 612 BC, in line with the prophecies of Nahum and Zephaniah, Nineveh was captured by a joint effort between the Babylonians and the Medes. The Egyptians marched north to assist the Assyrians but were soundly defeated by the Babylonians at the famous battle of Carchemish in 605 BC.

The fifth major invasion was in 605 BC when Nebuchadnezzar, the king of Babylon, having defeated the Assyrians, marched into Judah and besieged Jerusalem. He took treasures from the temple back to Babylon, along with some elite men of the city, including Daniel and his three friends. On this occasion, Nebuchadnezzar left the city standing.

In 597 BC, Nebuchadnezzar returned to Jerusalem, captured it, and took most of the inhabitants away to Babylon. Ezekiel was among them, and it was five years later, in Babylon, that he received his prophetic calling. Then the Hebrew world began to cave in.

The seventh invasion was the last time Nebuchadnezzar came to Jerusalem, in 588 BC. After a three-year siege, the city was taken. The Bible records, 'In the fifth month, on the seventh day of the month—that was the nineteenth year of King Nebuchadnezzar, king of Babylon—Nebuzaradan, the captain of the bodyguard, a servant of the king of Babylon, came to Jerusalem. And he burned the house of the LORD and the king's house and all the houses of Jerusalem; every great house he burned down. And all the army of the Chaldeans, who were with the captain of the guard, broke down the walls around Jerusalem' (2 Kings 25:8–10). The unspeakable had happened: the temple and the city were destroyed, people died and prophets cried.

Professor John Bright elucidated on the state of Israel and Judah, writing, 'Nebuchadnezzar's army left Judah a shambles. As archaeological evidence eloquently testifies, all, or virtually all, of the fortified cities in the heartland of Judah were razed to the ground... the population of the land was drained away.'[13]

This was a massive blow to the Hebrew psyche. God had allowed their land, their city and their temple to be taken and destroyed. Their shock was palpable. John Bright also wrote, 'The destruction of Jerusalem and the subsequent exile, mark the great watershed of Israel's history. At a stroke her national

---
[13] John Bright, *A History of Israel*, (SCM Press, London, 1972), p.344

existence was ended and, with it, all the institutions in which her corporate life had expressed itself; they would never be created in precisely the same form again.'[14]

No more journeying to Jerusalem for the great feasts, no more worship at the temple, no more sacrifices for personal and national sins at the great altar. It was all gone. Jerusalem had become a ghost town. An unknown psalmist wrote, 'By the waters of Babylon, there we sat down and wept, when we remembered Zion. On the willows there we hung up our lyres. For there our captors required of us songs, and our tormentors, mirth, saying, "Sing us one of the songs of Zion!" How shall we sing the LORD's song in a foreign land?' (Psalm 137:1–4). Jeremiah, the prophet, describes the utter destruction of Jerusalem in vivid terms in his aptly named *Lamentations*. However, there was a note of hope that emerged amid the despair.

The captive Hebrews now had to rethink their faith and how to express it. They began to gather in open air places and in homes, and the Sabbath turned into a weekly gathering to read the Scripture, to worship and to pray. This became a pattern that led the way into meeting for worship and teaching at the synagogue.

The Blessed Return

For 70 years the land was bereft. The Hebrews were scattered, feeling again the pain of being captive to another world power. To replace them, people from Mesopotamia were shipped in by the Assyrian administration, and they became thoroughly

---

[14] John Bright, *A History of Israel*, (SCM Press, London, 1972), p.343

ensconced in the land, marrying across racial boundaries, and eventually they became what we know as the Samaritans.

But there were glimmers of hope. Before the Exile had occurred, Jeremiah had prophesied, 'For thus says the LORD: When seventy years are completed for Babylon, I will visit you, and I will fulfil to you my promise and bring you back to this place' (Jeremiah 29:10). Later, in 539 BC, the Babylonian Empire was replaced by the Medo-Persian Empire. At that time, Daniel was prayerfully musing on the Scriptures. He recorded, 'In the first year of Darius the son of Ahasuerus, by descent a Mede, who was made king over the realm of the Chaldeans – in the first year of his reign, I, Daniel, perceived in the books the number of years that, according to the word of the LORD to Jeremiah the prophet, must pass before the end of the desolations of Jerusalem, namely, seventy years. Then I turned my face to the Lord God, seeking him by prayer and pleas for mercy with fasting and sackcloth and ashes' (Daniel 9:1–3).

Babylon fell to Cyrus, the king of Persia in 538 BC, and the following year, he authorised the first return to Jerusalem under the leadership of Sheshbazzar and Zerubbabel. Work began to restore worship, and the foundation of a new temple was laid. Delayed by the opposition of the Samaritans, an intervention by the Persian administration was needed before the new temple was finished in 515 BC. For several decades after, according to Professor R.K. Harrison, 'the Jews eked out a precarious living around Jerusalem and were at the mercy of anyone who chose to frustrate their humble designs.'[15]

---

[15] R. K. Harrison, *Old Testament Times*, (IVP, London, 1970), p.281

In 458 BC, the then Persian king, Artexerxes I, commissioned Ezra to go to Jerusalem to teach the Law and re-establish the true worship of God. Nehemiah joined him, 12 years later, carrying a burden to see the broken walls repaired. Remarkably, this was accomplished in just 52 days, despite continued local opposition. The nation was restored after 70 years of painful exile, and Israel never returned to idolatry.

The last prophet of the Old Testament was Malachi. Among other things, he prophesied a new day: 'Remember the law of my servant Moses, the statutes and rules that I commanded him at Horeb for all Israel. Behold, I will send you Elijah the prophet before the great and awesome day of the LORD comes. And he will turn the hearts of fathers to their children and the hearts of children to their fathers, lest I come and strike the land with a decree of utter destruction' (Malachi 4:4–6). Two individuals are mentioned – Moses and Elijah – who represent the Law and the Prophets.

The big story covered by the Old Testament comes to a close. Afterwards, there will be around 400 years of upheaval and spiritual darkness, radically changing the face of Israel.

Chapter 4

The Dark Pause in the Big Story

The Bit in Between

Before we break into the big story found in the New Testament, I think it is important to give our attention to another narrative that occurred during the 400 years mentioned in the previous chapter. This time is also known as the *inter-testamental period*. W. Graham Scroggie, a wonderful Bible expositor, wrote, 'The New Testament does not begin from where the Old Testament ends. Tremendous changes took place in all directions, and to know what these were, and what was their significance, is of the utmost importance for an understanding of how the story of the first hundred years AD was made possible.'[1]

This was a long epoch where prophetic voices fell silent, and the light of God ceased to shine on the nation. It was also a season of the seeming absence of God. Within that spiritual vacuum, a melting pot was formed, which strong voices and great powers began to stir. In the ensuing darkness, the

---

[1] W. Graham Scroggie, *The Unfolding Drama of Redemption, Vol.2* (Kregel Publications, Michigan, 1994), p.25

political, social and religious landscape heaved and buckled in response.

It's like God was spending a lot of time rearranging the stage, getting it ready for the second half of the story. After the first part ends, the interval curtain comes down to prepare for the second. The audience can see nothing, but behind the curtain, there is a lot of movement. When the curtains open again, the scene is totally different.

Political Developments

To imagine the time frame, consider the difference between the reigns of Elizabeth I and Elizabeth II. There were many significant changes in England during that particular 400-year period. So it was with Israel between the testaments. It is important to understand, because it is the background to all that Jesus and the early church experienced.

What happened during this period is not recorded in our canon of Scripture, but much information can be found in the Apocryphal books of 1 and 2 Maccabees. This narrative, although not recognised as a sacred text by most, is probably the best historical documentation of that period. We can also find much additional material in *The Antiquities of the Jews*, written by Flavius Josephus, a Jewish historian (AD 37–101).[2]

There is also a prophetic glimpse in the book of Daniel. When interpreting a dream for Nebuchadnezzar (Daniel 2:1–45), Daniel gave a strong, accurate, prophetic flash of insight into this period of history. Nebuchadnezzar's dream was of a statue – the head was made of gold, the chest and arms were

---

[2] See Flavius Josephus, *The Works of Flavius Josephus*, translated by William Whiston, (Nimmo, Hay & Mitchell, Edinburgh, 1895)

made of silver, its middle and thighs were made of bronze, and its feet were made of iron and clay. Daniel said the head of gold was Nebuchadnezzar, the present king of Babylon. He then outlined three other empires that would come after Babylon – the Medo-Persian Empire, the Greek Empire and the Roman Empire. The accuracy of Daniel's prediction is astonishing and remarkable.

The last Old Testament prophet, Malachi, prophesied under the rule of the Medo-Persian Empire, 'the chest and arms of silver' in Daniel's vision. This empire lasted for just over 200 years until, in 335 BC, Alexander the Great swept through the Mediterranean countries, pushing east as far as India. He was the 'middle and thighs of bronze'. During his time, he sowed Greek (Hellenist) culture into all the lands he conquered. Greek became the language of the day. Greek culture was essentially secular, although there was a religious side to it in 'the nodding of the head' to the Greek pantheon of gods. Polytheism ruled the day. (The apostle Paul would later encounter Greek culture and philosophy in Athens.)[3]

After the early death of Alexander the Great in 323 BC, the region experienced a power vacuum. Because he had no successor, four of Alexander's generals divided his vast empire among them. They were called the *Diadochoi* – the 'successors' – Seleucus, Lysimachus, Cassander and Ptolemy. Ptolemy took Egypt and then Judea. Over the decades that followed, Israel became a plundering ground and a theatre of war.

In 198 BC, the Seleucids (who ruled Mesopotamia and Persia) took control of Judea. They were defeated by the

---

[3] See Acts 17:16-32

Romans in 190 BC at the battle of Magnesia, in what is now modern-day Turkey, however, they continued to rule over Judea.

During this time, two historical figures stand out. The first is the Seleucid king, Antiochus IV Epiphanes (215–164 BC). Like several monarchs and emperors of this era, he had an over-inflated opinion of himself. He felt he was the visible manifestation of the Greek god Zeus. In the Jewish Museum in New York, there is a coin – a tetradrachm. On one side is an image of Antiochus and on the other side is an image of Zeus. The inscription reads, 'Of King Antiochus, god made manifest and victorious.'[4] Antiochus deposed the high priest Jason and set up his own man, Menelaus. However, whilst Antiochus was campaigning in Egypt, Jason, with 1000 soldiers rebelled, and made an attack on Jerusalem.

2 Maccabees 5:11–14 records of Antiochus that, 'raging like a wild animal, he set out from Egypt and took Jerusalem by storm. He ordered his soldiers to cut down without mercy those whom they met and to slay those who took refuge in their houses. There was a massacre of young and old, a killing of women and children, a slaughter of virgins and infants. In the space of three days, eighty thousand were lost, forty thousand meeting a violent death, and the same number being sold into slavery.' During this time, Antiochus also introduced a statue of Zeus into the temple.

Ray C. Stedman, writing of this event, says, 'When he forced his way into the Holy of Holies, he destroyed the scrolls of the Law and, to the absolute horror of the Jews, took a sow and

---

[4] Everett Ferguson, *Backgrounds of Early Christianity*, (Eerdmans, Michigan, 1987), p.322

offered it upon the sacred altar. Then with a broth made from the flesh of this unclean animal, he sprinkled everything in the temple, thus completely defiling and violating the sanctuary. It is impossible for us to grasp how horrifying this was to the Jews.'[5] Antiochus went even further by forbidding circumcision, the keeping of the Sabbath and even the reading of the Law. The religious life of Israel was being systematically obliterated, and their suffering was intense. Under this severe religious and social oppression, deep resentments began to simmer.

The Maccabean family (the name Maccabee means 'the hammer') rose in anger, raised an army, and in a series of pitched battles, in which they were always the minority, ousted the oppressors in 164 BC. They were led firstly by the priest Mattathias, who was succeeded within a year by his son Judas Maccabaeus. The temple was first cleansed, then re-dedicated and the worship of God resumed. The Jews still celebrate this event, calling it Hanukkah: 'The dedication,' or, the festival of lights.

In 142 BC, Jewish independence was recognised by the Seleucids, and rule passed to the Maccabean family. Simon was named high priest and commander and leader of Judea. This was the beginning of the Hasmonean dynasty.

In 64–63 BC, civil war broke out between two Hasmonean brothers, Aristobulus and Hyrcanus. Rome was in the wings, like a hawk – watching and waiting. Things deteriorated so badly that both brothers asked Rome to intervene. They were

---

[5] Ray Stedman, 'The 400 Years between the Old and New Testaments', www.RayStedman.org

betrayed by a priest, who opened the door for the Romans to settle the many battles taking place.

Here we introduce the second of our historical figures – the Roman General Pompey. He was a leading Roman commander and a great statesman. He was instrumental in Rome's transformation from a Republic to an Empire.

In responding to the above request for help, there were attempts to bring some kind of order. Then, in the face of a stand-off with Jewish fanatics who had seized the temple mount, Pompey entered Jerusalem, 'overthrew the city and captured it for Rome.'[6] He destroyed part of the sacred temple and desecrated the most holy place – another deep blow and insult to the Jewish heart. 'From that time on, Palestine was under the authority and power of Rome.'[7] The Roman Empire was the last kingdom in Daniel's vision – the one 'made of iron and clay'.

We now enter a world stage where Rome is everywhere, exerting her authority. The 'Pax Romana' was a 'peace' that was both felt and enforced. Professor Edwin Judge, an expert in ancient biblical history wrote, 'the creation of a Roman province... neither suspended existing governments nor added to the Roman state. The Governor worked in association with friendly powers in the area to preserve Rome's military security...'[8] Each state could negotiate its own rights and privileges. While Judea theoretically remained autonomous, it

---

[6] Ray Stedman, 'The 400 Years between the Old and New Testaments', www.RayStedman.org
[7] Ibid.
[8] E.A. Judge, *Roman Empire*, New Bible Dictionary, (Inter-Varsity Press, London, 1970), p.1100

was obliged to pay tribute to, and depend on, the Roman administration.

In 37 BC, Rome appointed Herod the Great, an Idumaean, to be the king of the Jews. Around 19 BC, he began rebuilding the temple. It was a magnificent structure but utterly devoid of the presence of God. Herod was a monster, murdering some of his own wives and children. Caesar Augustus, a friend of Herod, is claimed to have said, 'I would rather be Herod's pig than his son.'

Dr Bob Duerden, my friend who has spent hours editing this book, wrote in a letter, 'The medico-historical evidence suggests that Herod probably suffered from hypothyroidic disorder, a condition which makes the person very suspicious of those around them... a dangerous disease for kings and emperors to have – at least, for those close to them.' We can think of many national leaders who over the years have exhibited these symptoms!

At this juncture, it would be worth mentioning the timeline of the Herodian kings, though they span beyond the intertestamental period. Herod the Great (reigned 37–4 BC) was the master builder, seeking to replicate Rome in Judea. He built the temple, seven palaces (each of them larger than anything the Caesars had in Rome), fortresses, viaducts, amphitheatres, etc.

It was this Herod in whose reign Jesus was born (See page 100 for more explanation). He received the wise men, slaughtered the infant boys at Bethlehem and died in Jericho after an excruciatingly painful and putrefying illness.

He was succeeded by his eldest son, Archelaus (reigned 4 BC–AD 6). Archelaus was not a king as such, but an ethnarch (a political leader over a common ethnic group). He oversaw Judea, Samaria, and Idumea. It was under his despotic rule that Joseph and Mary relocated to Galilee. He was eventually banished by Caesar Augustus to Gaul (France).

Then came Herod Antipas, the youngest son of Herod the Great. He became the tetrarch (ruler of a quarter – one of four appointed regional rulers) of Galilee and Perea from 4 BC to AD 39. It was this Herod whom Jesus referred to as 'that fox' (Luke 13:32), who murdered John the Baptist (Matthew 14:10) and who had a brief encounter with Jesus during His trial (Luke 23:7–12). He was denounced by his nephew Agrippa and eventually exiled to Spain by the Emperor Caligula.

Agrippa took the title of Herod Agrippa I. He was a grandson of Herod the Great, and he reigned from AD 41 to 44. It was he who had James the disciple put to death (Acts 12:2). He died suddenly, slain by an angel of God (Acts 12:23). He left one son and two daughters, Bernice and Drusilla. (Both these daughters are mentioned in Acts – Drusilla is the wife of Governor Felix in Acts 24:24, and Bernice attended Paul's trial in Acts 25:13,23 and 26:30).

The son was called Herod Agrippa II. He was too young to succeed his father at first, but in AD 53, he was granted rule of the northern territories, and a year later, rule over Galilee and Perea. It was this Agrippa who heard the apostle Paul's defence (Acts 25:13–26:32).

Spiritual Developments

During the intertestamental era, several other significant things took place. Around 280–250 BC, the Hebrew Bible was translated into Greek, called the Septuagint. It would have been used extensively by Jesus, the apostles and Paul.

Factions also emerged within the priesthood. According to Josephus, around 160 BC, three schools of thought emerged: the Pharisees, the Sadducees and the Essenes.

The **Pharisees** probably emerged from the *Hasidim* – 'the godly people.' This was a group of people who, some decades after the return from Exile, banded together to encourage the study and practice of the sacred Law in the midst of perceived moral and spiritual decline.[9] The Pharisees were the largest and most influential of the groups.

Their name was derived from the Hebrew word *parash* which meant 'to separate.' They were the separatists – the 'Puritans' of the day. F.F. Bruce wrote, 'They deplored the inroads of Hellenistic ways into Jewish life... and were despised as antiquated spoil-sports by those of the younger generation, even within priestly families, who ardently accepted the new fashion.'[10] This zeal for the Scriptures over the years sadly turned into an ultra-protectionism for the *Torah* – the Law of God. Out of them grew different groups, some being stricter than others. The school of Shammai and the school of Hillel were the most prominent.

The Pharisees were strict adherents to the whole Law of Moses, constructing the *Talmud* to protect the Law. Merrill

---

[9] See F.F. Bruce, *Paul – Apostle of the Free Spirit*, (Paternoster Press, Exeter, 1977), p.44
[10] Ibid, p.45

Tenney wrote, 'They believed in the existence of angels, in the immortality of the soul and in the resurrection of the dead. They practised ritual prayer and fasting and tithed their property meticulously. They kept the Sabbath very strictly, allowing not even for the healing of the sick, nor for the casual plucking of grain for eating by the roadside.'[11]

Eugene Peterson provided a beautiful metaphor for this over-protectiveness.[12] He described a large window revealing a panoramic view of mountains, lakes and forests. It was the greatest pride of the owner, and he was diligent to keep it pristine. However, over time, bird droppings began to mar the window, and then children's dirty fingerprints. It needed constant cleaning. In his zeal to keep it clean, the owner eventually boarded the window up to prevent it being soiled again. It is unmarked, but no one can see the beautiful views anymore!

The second group were the **Sadducees**. Tradition has it that their name derived from the sons of Zadok, who was high priest during the reigns of David and Solomon. The Sadducees had political power and were the governing group under the reign of the Herods. They held onto the office of high priest and held sway in the Sanhedrin, which was the supreme Jewish legislative and judicial court in Jerusalem. *The New Bible Dictionary* notes that:

> In religion, the Sadducees are marked for their conservatism. They denied the permanent validity of any but the written laws of the Pentateuch. They

---
[11] Merrill C. Tenney, *New Testament Survey*, (IVP, London, 1973), p.110
[12] Eugene Peterson, *The Jesus Way*, (Hodder & Stoughton, London, 2007), p.211

> rejected the later doctrines of the soul and the afterlife, the resurrection, rewards and retributions, angels and demons. They believed that there was no fate, men having a free choice of good and evil, prosperity and adversity being the outcome of their own course of action.[13]

As anti-supernaturalists, they were coldly ethical and literal and were wide open to Hellenistic influences. They were opportunists who were quite ready to change sides to maintain their power and prestige. They collaborated with their Roman overlords, being fearful of rocking any boats. For those reasons, they were very nervous of anything or anyone who upset the status quo.

The third group were the **Essenes**. They were the spiritual radicals of the day. They refused to have anything to do with the temple because of the widespread corruption found within its precincts. They committed themselves to studying and copying the Scriptures. They lived simply, focusing on personal purity, both inner and outer. They were highly disciplined, extremely focused and had little to no patience with spiritual or social compromises.

Their watchword is found in Isaiah 40:3: 'In the wilderness prepare the way of the LORD; make straight in the desert a highway for our God.' Having rejected the corruption of the Jerusalem temple, they established monastic-like communities in and around Judea. The discovery of the Dead Sea Scrolls is almost certainly related to the preserving work of the Essene community in Khirbet Qumran, eight miles south of Jericho.

---

[13] A. Gelston, *Sadducees*, New Bible Dictionary, (IVP, London, 1970), p.1124

Three other significant societal groups emerged during this time. One of them was the **Herodians**. They are termed 'the enemies of Christ' mentioned only in Mark's Gospel (Mark 3:6; 12:13). The Jewish historian Josephus made mention of them as loyal supporters of the Herodian dynasty. They were not a religious group as such, but a collection of influential people sympathetic to Rome.

There were also the **Hellenists**. These were Greek-speaking Jews from all over the Roman world – the Jewish diaspora. They were far more liberal in their approach and had adopted the Greek language and Greek ways. They were noted for their overly pragmatic views, adapting the prevailing culture into their own to such an extent that they lost their distinctives. The moral high ground of Judaism was largely lost among them, and they met in their own synagogues.

Finally, there were the **Zealots**. These were fanatical nationalists who held that there was no king except God. They advocated violence as a means of freeing the country from the grip of Rome. Passionate for justice and fairness, they cared about the exploited, the victims and the persecuted. 'They had a vision of a better world, and they were ready to die for it.'[14]

Into this dark cesspit came a long-awaited light. The prophet Daniel had said, 'And in the days of those kings the God of heaven will set up a kingdom that shall never be destroyed, nor shall the kingdom be left to another people. It shall break in pieces all these kingdoms and bring them to an end, and it shall stand forever, just as you saw that a stone was cut from a mountain by no human hand, and that it broke in pieces the

---

[14] Eugene Peterson, *The Jesus Way*, (Hodder & Stoughton, London, 2007), pp.254,256

iron, the bronze, the clay, the silver, and the gold' (Daniel 2:44, 45). The stone that was cut by no human hand, the one that broke all the other kingdoms, the kingdom that will never end, was none other than the kingdom of Jesus Christ, the Messiah. He was the stone rejected by the leadership of the day, and yet His kingdom would overtake all others and reign forever (Matthew 21:42–44).

Conclusions

The Israel that Jesus was born into was almost unrecognisable from that of the Old Testament. The Roman world had introduced an enforced political stability, but also a lifestyle of deep and dreadful moral decadence. Hedonism (living for pleasure) ruled unabated. This had been resisted by conservative and zealous Jews. At times there had even been revolt. A deep despair over the land mingled with profound disillusionment regarding the religious and political status quo. People, sickened with what they saw and experienced around them, yearned for something more; something clean and upright.

Throughout the Mediterranean coastlands, the Greek language had been introduced by Alexander, and a Greek translation of the Old Testament had been produced. It paved the way for not only the Jewish nation, but other nations to hear the Word of God. It would become an incredible asset for the advancement of the gospel.

The Roman Empire had sought to unite the world under a single government, managed locally. Rome loved to build. They built bridges, viaducts and roads that interlinked many cities, making travel faster, easier and safer. It provided a tremendous communication system for the gospel.

The apostle Paul, writing years later, said, 'But when the fullness of time had come, God sent forth his Son, born of woman...' (Galatians 4:4). God's providence had prepared the stage for the next part of His redemptive story.

Chapter 5

The Big Story in the New Testament

The Light Emerges

Deep within the Old Testament Scriptures lie hundreds of far-sighted prophetic pointers regarding the hope of the nations: The Messiah – The Anointed One. They lay hidden for centuries, seen only by prophetic eyes. One of these prophets was Isaiah: 'The people who walked in darkness have seen a great light; those who dwelt in a land of deep darkness, on them has light shone' (Isaiah 9:2). That light was ready to emerge.

The last prophet of the Old Testament, Malachi, prophesied, 'Behold, I will send you Elijah the prophet before the great and awesome day of the LORD comes. And he will turn the hearts of fathers to their children and the hearts of children to their fathers' (Malachi 4:5). Centuries later, an Elijah-like man walks out of the wilderness with Isaiah's strong prophetic message 'Prepare the way of the Lord!' (Isaiah 40:3) pulsing in his heart. His name was John, and he became known as John the Baptist. This is the story of his birth.

Roughly 400 years after Malachi's prophecy, an aged priest called Zechariah was on duty in the temple in Jerusalem. He was startled by the sudden appearance of the Archangel Gabriel, who told him that, after decades of barrenness, his wife was going to have a son:

> Do not be afraid, Zechariah, for your prayer has been heard, and your wife Elizabeth will bear you a son, and you shall call his name John. And you will have joy and gladness, and many will rejoice at his birth, for he will be great before the Lord. And he must not drink wine or strong drink, and he will be filled with the Holy Spirit, even from his mother's womb. And he will turn many of the children of Israel to the Lord their God, and he will go before him in the spirit and power of Elijah, to turn the hearts of the fathers to the children, and the disobedient to the wisdom of the just, to make ready for the Lord a people prepared (Luke 1:13–17).

John was a miracle baby with a prophetic destiny. Zechariah, his father, prophesied at his birth: 'And you, child, will be called the prophet of the Most High; for you will go before the Lord to prepare his ways, to give knowledge of salvation to his people in the forgiveness of their sins' (Luke 1:76,77).

It is highly possible that his aged parents died when he was young. Research suggests he was probably taken in and adopted by the Essenes, who lived in the wilderness and had a practice of taking in orphan boys and raising them up in the ways of the Lord.

Let us now think about the birth of Jesus. Some six months after John's conception, the Archangel Gabriel came to a young virgin called Mary, engaged to be married, and gave her some tremendous and life-changing news. Luke recorded the encounter:

> And he came to her and said, 'Greetings, O favoured one, the Lord is with you!' But she was greatly troubled at the saying, and tried to discern what sort of greeting this might be. And the angel said to her, 'Do not be afraid, Mary, for you have found favour with God. And behold, you will conceive in your womb and bear a son, and you shall call his name Jesus. He will be great and will be called the Son of the Most High. And the Lord God will give to him the throne of his father David, and he will reign over the house of Jacob forever, and of his kingdom there will be no end' (Luke 1:28–33).

Mary probably had an awful job trying to convince Joseph, her betrothed, but God spoke to him in a powerful dream (Matthew 1:19–15). In fact, the whole birth narrative was surrounded by dreams, angelic visitations, prophetic words and strange visits by rough shepherds and Persian magicians to name a few.

This birth was another miracle birth, but of a sort not seen before. It was a work of the Holy Spirit. The virgin birth of Jesus is a cardinal truth of the Christian faith. He had to be born of a woman, but not of a man (Isaiah 7:14). Joseph, therefore, was not the father of Jesus – he fostered Him, accepting Him as his son. Remember our earlier discussion about the effects of Adam's sin being passed on to the whole human race? To bring about our salvation, the promised Messiah could not have the virulent seed of Adamic nature in Him.

James Leo Garrett Jr, a Distinguished Professor of Theology Emeritus at Southwestern Baptist Theological Seminary, wrote regarding the virgin birth, 'To be the Redeemer of mankind, Jesus must identify himself with human beings and at the same time transcend the human race.'[1]

Concerning the timing of His birth, a sensible dating puts it around 5 BC. From the Scriptures, we can see that Jesus was born just after the time of the census which took place around 8 BC and before the death of Herod which occurred in 4 BC.

It is also to be noted that Jesus was not born on the 25 December. The Scriptures tell us that shepherds were watching their flock by night when the angel visited them with the news that the child had been born in Bethlehem. In Judea, flocks of sheep were taken out to pasture around the time of Passover in the Hebrew month of Abib (around March or April) and stayed out until the onset of winter (October). Jesus was born, therefore, somewhere between March and October. Our date for Christmas was assigned much later by the Romans.

At the age of 12, Jesus went with Joseph and Mary to Jerusalem to be presented to the Lord and, during that time, went 'missing'. He was eventually found in the temple, debating with the teachers. When questioned, the boy Jesus replied, 'Why were you looking for me? Did you not know that I must be in my Father's house?' (Luke 2:49) It seems that Jesus truly understood that God was His Father, and not Joseph. After that, He returned to Nazareth with Joseph and Mary 'and was

---

[1] James Leo Garrett Jr, *Systematic Theology*, Vol. 1, (Bibal Press, Texas, 2007), p.682

submissive to them' (Luke 2:51). When we read this, we have a reminder that the power of God is manifested through those who are under authority. This was recognised by a Roman centurion years later (Matthew 8:5–10).

For the next 18 years or so, Jesus grew up in His home in Nazareth, apprenticed to Joseph, learning the trade of an artisan. The word 'carpenter' comes from the Greek word *tektōn*, and really describes a craftsman. Jesus would have worked, not only with wood, but possibly with stone and metal as well. Mary and Joseph went on to have other children. Matthew names the younger brothers of Jesus as James, Joseph, Simon and Judas, and then there were His unnamed sisters (Matthew 13:55). The Gospel narrative tells us that during this time, and throughout His ministry, His brothers did not believe in Him (John 7:5).

It was only after the Resurrection that they recognised who He really was, and His half-brother James later became the leader of the church in Jerusalem.

The Light Manifests

We now return to John the Baptist. Some years later, around AD 29 (Luke is quite precise about the dating – 'the fifteenth year of Tiberius Caesar' – Luke 3:1,2), he emerged from the wilderness of Judea, wearing 'a garment of camel hair and a leather belt around his waist, and his food was locusts and wild honey' (Matthew 3:4). He then began to 'proclaim a baptism of repentance for the forgiveness of sins' (Luke 3:3). He quickly attracted a following of those disillusioned with the religious status quo, and desperate for an authentic spirituality. He also attracted the notice of the religious leaders and even some Roman soldiers.

Around this time, Jesus walked from Galilee to the River Jordan, where John was baptising, and requested that John baptise Him. John looked intently at Him and, under the inspiration of the Spirit, said to those around him, 'Behold, the Lamb of God, who takes away the sin of the world!' (John 1:29). This statement is profound. In one brief sentence, John summed up the whole thrust of the Hebrew sacrificial system. He saw that the principle of an innocent (lamb) dying for those who were guilty of sin was now being fulfilled for all humanity in one man. Remember, this principle was first set in place in Genesis, and then enacted out by the Hebrew nation over hundreds of years in their sacrificial systems and in their worship of God.

I am reminded of the words of Aslan to Susan and Lucy in the story *The Lion, the Witch and the Wardrobe*, when they realised that Aslan was alive after being brutally killed by the white witch. Susan asked Aslan, 'But what does it all mean?'

> "It means," said Aslan, "that though the Witch knew the Deep Magic, there is a magic deeper still which she did not know. Her knowledge goes back only to the dawn of time. But if she could have looked a little further back, into the stillness and the darkness before Time dawned, she would have read there a different incantation. She would have known that when a willing victim who had committed no treachery was killed in a traitor's stead, the Table would crack and Death itself would start working backwards."[2]

---

[2] C.S. Lewis, *The Lion, the Witch and the Wardrobe*, (Grafton, London, 2002), p.148

Tom Wright wrote, 'In other words, the powers that put Jesus on the cross didn't realise that by doing so they were in fact serving God's purposes, unveiling the wisdom that lies at the heart of the universe.'[3]

As Jesus stepped out of the water after being baptised, the heavens suddenly opened, and the Spirit of the Lord came down upon Him in the form of a dove and rested on Him. Then came the voice of the Father saying, 'This is my beloved Son, with whom I am well pleased' (Matthew 3:17). The light of heaven had come to the sin-darkened earth.

Suddenly, He felt the propelling hand of the Spirit driving Him into the wilderness of Judea. He remained there, fasting, for 40 days. Towards the end of this period, Satan came to Him, seeking to throw Him off track, but was totally unsuccessful. 'And when the devil had ended every temptation, he departed from him until an opportune time. And Jesus returned in the power of the Spirit to Galilee, and a report about him went out through all the surrounding country' (Luke 4:13–14).

Then Jesus began His ministry, which consisted firstly of preaching and teaching about the kingdom of God, and secondly of ministering healing and deliverance to the sick and demonised. As He taught, He revealed His Father's heart for people. The signs and wonders pointed to His Father's compassion and power. Never had this sort of ministry been witnessed before, and Jesus began to draw huge crowds.

Around this time, Jesus chose 12 disciples, who became the first apostles. It is worth noting that these men came from diverse backgrounds and had different temperaments. One can

---

[3] Tom Wright, *How God became King*, (SPCK, London, 2012), p.205

only imagine how Simon the Zealot got on with Matthew the tax collector! Yet, such would be the essence of the church that would later emerge. William Barclay wrote, 'Christianity began by insisting that the most diverse people should live together and by enabling them to do so, because they were all living with Jesus.'[4]

Jesus spent a lot of time with these men, investing deeply into their lives and preparing them for their future ministries. Barclay put it this way: 'If they were to do His work in the world, they must live in His presence, before they went out into the world; they must go from the presence of Jesus to the presence of men... no work of Christ can ever be done except by him who comes from the presence of Christ.'[5]

Jesus came, however, not just to preach or to heal, but to die. This was His purpose throughout. His whole life was to be a fulfilment of the prophetic strains scattered throughout the Old Testament Scriptures. When Jesus met with two disciples walking disconsolately back to Emmaus after His death and Resurrection, He said, 'O foolish ones, and slow of heart to believe *all that the prophets* have spoken! Was it not necessary that the Christ should suffer these things and enter into his glory? And *beginning with Moses and all the Prophets*, he interpreted to them in all the Scriptures the things concerning himself' (Luke 24:25–27; emphasis mine).

Later that day, to the disciples in the upper room, Jesus said, 'These are my words that I spoke to you while I was still

---

[4] William Barclay, *The Gospel of Mark*, The Daily Study Bible, (St Andrew Press, Edinburgh, 1975), p.74
[5] William Barclay, *The Gospel of Matthew, Vol 1*, The Daily Study Bible, (St Andrew Press, Edinburgh, 1975), p.361

with you, *that everything written about me in the Law of Moses and the Prophets and the Psalms* must be fulfilled' (Luke 24: 44; emphasis mine).

Much of the narrative in the gospels is taken up with what is called the Passion and Triumph of Christ – His arrest, trial and crucifixion, followed by His Resurrection and Ascension back into heaven. His death on the Cross was the great demonstration that an innocent lamb died for the guilty, and His Resurrection was the confirmation from God that the virus of sin had been dealt a fatal blow, being atoned for once and for all. This was the big purpose of His coming. When facing it in Gethsemane, He said in His anguished prayer, 'Now is my soul troubled. And what shall I say? "Father, save me from this hour?" But for this purpose I have come to this hour' (John 12:27).

We must remember: there was another domain that was, and still is, at perpetual war with everything God says and does. Satanic strategies are permanently set against everything God has purposed. Especially loathed are the sons and daughters of Adam and Eve. Hated even more is Jesus, the eternal Son of God, who came to restore and reconcile the human race back to the Father. At some point these two worlds were going to clash, and clash violently. As usual, Satan would work through human agencies.

In his book, *How God became King*, Tom Wright explained it this way: 'The accuser, working through Judas, will draw the enemy fire onto Jesus… Jesus' followers are to understand the horrible events of the next twenty-four hours as a battle reaching its height, a battle with the real enemy who is working through the treachery of Judas and the callous power of Rome.'[6]

On many occasions, Jesus sought to warn His disciples about what was going to happen to Him, but they didn't heed Him. His message grew increasingly stark until, 'as Jesus was going up to Jerusalem, he took the twelve disciples aside, and on the way he said to them, "See, we are going up to Jerusalem. And the Son of Man will be delivered over to the chief priests and scribes, and they will condemn him to death and deliver him over to the Gentiles to be mocked and flogged and crucified, and he will be raised on the third day"' (Matthew 20:17–19).

Then the moment of darkness came. Satan entered Judas Iscariot, one of the 12, and Jesus was betrayed by him to the Jewish authorities. After an illegal trial, Jesus was surrendered to the Roman authorities on a charge of blasphemy. Pontius Pilate declared three times that he found no guilt in Jesus. Nevertheless, the Jewish authorities pressed harder, and Pilate capitulated, sentencing Him to death by crucifixion.

This was a cruel and humiliating form of execution. Stripped naked, the victim was either tied or nailed to a cross, which was then hauled up, and dropped into place. Death came after several hours, if not days. The Roman orator, Cicero, described crucifixion as 'a most cruel and disgusting punishment,'[7] and Josephus called it 'the most wretched of deaths.'[8]

---

[6] Tom Wright, *How God became King*, (SPCK, New York, 2012), p.142
[7] Cicero, *Against Verres II.v.64*. paragraph 165
[8] Josephus *Jewish War*. 7.203.

One of the most profound Scriptures in the New Testament is found in Paul's second letter to the church in Corinth. He wrote, 'For our sake he made him to be sin who knew no sin' (2 Corinthians 5:21). Here we tread reverently, trying to peer into a deep mystery. My feelings are that all sin was gathered from all time to a single moment in time, into a single place, upon a single man, on a single day. From ages past, present and even from the future, the cancer of sin came and centred itself on Jesus. Like a writhing dark evil, it wrapped itself around Him, soaking and staining Him with its horrendous stench. Everything in Him would have recoiled. Wayne Grudem writes, 'All that he hated most deeply was poured out fully upon him. And at that precise moment, the anger of God fell, and Jesus took the full brunt of it all.'[9] The heavens were darkened for three hours, and, in my view, it was a mercy. What was on the Cross at that point, was too hideous to behold.

Then Jesus said, 'It is finished' (John 19:30). The word He used was *teteléstai*, which means, 'to bring to a close, to finish, to bring to an end, to perform, to execute, to complete, to fulfil.' In my own view, it's as if He said, 'I have executed the great designs of the Almighty – I have satisfied the demands of His justice. I have accomplished all that was written in the Prophets, and suffered the utmost malice of my enemies; and now the way to the presence of God in the Holy of Holies is made manifest through My blood.'

Then Jesus' body was taken from the cross and buried. There it remained through Saturday.

---

[9] Wayne Grudem, *Systematic Theology*, (IVP, Leicester, 1994), p. 573

Early on the first day of the week, the unbelievable happened. Women came to the tomb where Jesus had been buried, to find the stone rolled away and the tomb empty. They reported this back to the disciples, who were hiding in fear of the Jewish authorities. Peter and John ran together to the tomb, saw it was indeed empty, and returned to the Upper Room. One of the women, Mary, lingered. She first saw two angels, and then she saw the risen Jesus. A short time afterwards, He showed Himself to the disciples. The shock, mingled with joy, sent them all into a spin.

The bodily Resurrection of Jesus became one of the cardinal doctrines of the church. Along with the Cross, it was a core subject in the apostles' preaching. Both the death and the Resurrection of Jesus also marked a dramatic change in the spiritual world. The power of sin and the power of death had been broken once and for all. Something new had been unleashed into the world – full forgiveness and a new and dynamic way of living. Our faith is constructed and sustained by these truths. The Resurrection is the endorsement of heaven that Jesus' work on the Cross was totally effective. Paul taught that, 'If Christ has not been raised, your faith is futile; you are still in your sins' (1 Corinthians 15:17).

After His Resurrection, Jesus spent around 40 days with the disciples, teaching them more about the kingdom of heaven. At the end of that time, He took them to Bethany, on the Mount of Olives. He told them to return to the city of Jerusalem to wait for the promise of the Spirit when they would be 'clothed with power from on high' (Luke 24:49). Immediately after uttering these words, He was suddenly lifted up 'and was carried into heaven' (Luke 24:51).

The Son of God re-entered the heaven He came from and took His seat at the right hand of the Father.

The Birth of the Church

At the Hebrew Feast of Weeks, *Shavuot,* known to us as Pentecost (held 50 days after Passover), the disciples were gathered in an upper room, praying and waiting on God. 'And suddenly there came from heaven a sound like a mighty rushing wind, and it filled the entire house where they were sitting. And divided tongues as of fire appeared to them and rested on each one of them. And they were all filled with the Holy Spirit and began to speak in other tongues as the Spirit gave them utterance' (Acts 2:2–4). At that moment, the church was born.

Peter, utterly transformed and emboldened, stepped out and preached to the gathered crowd with astonishing results. 3,000 people came to faith in Christ and were baptised. The mission had started. It spread like wildfire through the city. Miracles of healing began to happen, the church multiplied, and started to organise itself. Luke wrote, 'And they devoted themselves to the apostles' teaching and the fellowship, to the breaking of bread and the prayers. And awe came upon every soul, and many wonders and signs were being done through the apostles' (Acts 2:42,43).

It ran into trouble with the authorities, however, and soon there were martyrdoms. The first was of Stephen, one of the seven deacons. In addition to helping with food distribution, he testified and saw God's power manifest in miraculous signs of healing among the people. Hauled before the Jewish authorities on trumped up charges, he was asked to speak in his defence. Stephen gave a rousing overview of Hebrew history, and then pointed out their persistent resistance to the work of the Holy Spirit. Outraged by this, the authorities cast him out of the city and stoned him to death. Blood was spilt for the first time for Jesus' sake.

Saul of Tarsus

At this point, our attention is drawn to a young man named Saul. He was guarding the garments of those who were stoning Stephen. Luke wrote quite tersely, 'And Saul approved of his execution' (Acts 8:1). Saul was originally from Tarsus, a large city of about half a million, ten miles inland from the coast in Asia Minor (modern-day Turkey). Under Roman rule, Tarsus was the capital of East Cilicia. It was where Mark Antony first met Cleopatra. A city that pursued culture and learning.

Such was the case with Saul. In his own words, he was a pedigree Hebrew and a zealous Pharisee who had come to Jerusalem to study at the feet of the great Rabbi Gamaliel (Acts 22:3). It was here that he encountered first-hand the startling growth of the Christian church. The roots of it – the belief in the death and subsequent Resurrection of the man Jesus, purported to be the Messiah – shocked and disgusted him. When it came to the stoning of Stephen, Saul held the garments of those who stoned him to death, demonstrating his approval of the killing.

From that point, a rage against these people erupted in Saul. All the zeal of a Pharisee and the loyalty of a zealot combined to create an unquenchable inferno within him. He took his opposition to extremes, chasing down the believers and committing them to prison and death. In later years he would speak of his 'breathing threats and murder' (Acts 9:1) and 'the 'raging fury' that consumed him (Acts 26:11). *The Message* captures it perfectly: 'I stormed through their meeting places, bullying them into cursing Jesus, a one-man terror obsessed with obliterating these people' (Acts 26:11). To the Galatian believers he confessed, 'I persecuted the church of God violently and tried to destroy it' (Galatians 1:13).

Saul felt that this new sect was like a disease, threatening the religious life of Judaism. If it wasn't nipped in the bud, it would spread like a cancer. After wreaking havoc among the believers in Jerusalem, Saul turned his attention further afield. Obtaining letters from the religious rulers in Jerusalem, he made his way north to Damascus to arrest more followers of this new movement.

Then Jesus stepped in. Just outside Damascus, Saul was stopped in his tracks by a blinding light that threw him face down on the ground. He then heard Jesus speaking to him, 'Saul, Saul, why are you persecuting me?' (Acts 9:4) The experience shook Saul to the core of his being.

This encounter revealed two things: firstly, it showed there is no heart too hard, no mindset too fixed, and no path of destruction too determined that God cannot break in and transform it. Secondly, it demonstrated that the Christian faith is not just another set of beliefs, but a startling and life-changing revelation from heaven.

Writing much later to the church in Philippi, Saul, now Paul the apostle, described this experience as being 'apprehended' by Jesus whilst approaching the city (Philippians 3:12). The Greek word here is *katalambano*, and literally means 'to take hold of by the hand, pulling one down'. It seems that, as Saul chased after the followers of the Way, Jesus chased after him and wrestled him to the ground. The best way to see this is to imagine a rugby tackle!

Jesus blinded his spiritual darkness with light, and then gave him a revelation about the body of Christ – the church – with His words. In essence, Jesus said to him, 'In touching the church, you touch Me.'

Still blind, Saul was then led to Damascus by his terrified companions, where he took shelter in the house of a man called Judas, who lived in 'the street called Straight' (Acts 9:9–11). Incidentally, the name of that street still survives today in the Arabic form: Darb al-Mustaqim.

Saul was frightened and wretched. He did not eat or drink for three days, but sat in silence in the guest room. During those darkened hours, he began to realise the depths of what he had been doing.

Who knows the tearful conversations he had with the Lord during those three dark days? He would have grappled with guilt and remorse. The religious constructs of his mind, meticulously put together as a young student of Judaism, were disintegrating before his eyes. The Damascus Road experience was the beginning of a total unravelling of his previous mindset, and the starting point of a profound revelation of Jesus Christ.

God then sent a man called Ananias to pray for him. Saul's eyes miraculously opened, he was baptised in water and was filled with the Spirit.

A transformed Saul began his mission in earnest. He immediately began to preach in the synagogues in Damascus, but not for long. The zeal that had driven him to pursue Christians returned with renewed strength, only this time, it was a zeal for the name of Jesus! He started to proclaim that Jesus was the Son of God, sharing the story of his conversion. The representative of the high priest in Jerusalem had now become a representative of Jesus Christ, the Messiah. The audience was stunned. Soon, their shock turned to anger. After a threat on his life, he escaped at night by being let down in a basket through an opening in the wall.

At this point, the chronology of events is difficult to pin down and we need to compare the account in Acts, written by Luke (Acts 9:20-30), with Paul's own account in the opening verses of his letter to the Galatians (Galatians 1:11-2:10). Many theologians and scholars have studied these accounts, and the consensus is as follows.

It seems that from Damascus, Saul went into Arabia to Mount Sinai. This is where God had met with Moses and given him the Ten Commandments. It was also where Elijah journeyed to after Jezebel threatened to kill him. A place of covenant and restoration. It seems that Saul went there – back to the source, as it were.

It was not, however, a fleeting visit. He remained up to three long years in the silence and solitude of the desert. It is probable he was given the hospitality of nomadic tribes that encircled the vast area, but for most of the time, was alone with his thoughts and prayers.

During those three years of solitude and silence, Saul came face to face with the risen Jesus again, and saw himself in God's searching light, realising his own sinfulness. He writes in Galatians, 'the gospel that was preached by me is not man's gospel. For I did not receive it from any man, nor was I taught it, but I received it through a revelation of Jesus Christ' (Galatians 1:11b–12).

Saul realised that all his zeal and achievements in Judaism were meaningless. There must have been many hours of weeping as the last remaining bricks of his Pharisaic edifice were broken down. Although Saul had read and memorised the Scriptures from an early age, he had not seen or understood them from heaven's point of view. After the deconstruction, rebuilding was needed.

Much later, he wrote to the church in Corinth, describing a time where he was caught up in the Spirit to the third heaven, where he was exposed to 'visions and revelations of the Lord' (2 Corinthians 12:1), and where he 'heard things that cannot be told, which man may not utter' (2 Corinthians 12:4). This is better translated 'heard unspeakable words' – things that were impossible to relay – for no human terminology could adequately translate these visionary imprints of the Spirit. From these encounters came profound revelations, much of his theology concerning Christ and the church, and a renewed understanding of the Hebrew Scriptures. Saul was taught it by Jesus Himself.

After returning to Damascus, Saul then made his way to Jerusalem. As he entered the city, he encountered fearful suspicion by the church. He was eventually accepted, however, thanks to the help of a man called Barnabas.

Saul began to preach in Jerusalem, but he soon found himself stirring up more trouble. Concerning the church in Jerusalem, F.F. Bruce wrote, 'Paul in his persecuting days had been a thorn in their flesh, but they were to learn that Paul the Christian could also be a disturbing presence, and trouble was liable to break out every time he visited Jerusalem.'[10] Seeing the possibility of a further attempt on his life, his friends took him down to Caesarea, and sent him back to his home town in Tarsus in the region of Cilicia. Paul himself later refers to this time in his letter to the Galatians: 'Then I went into the regions of Syria and Cilicia. And I was still unknown in person to the churches of Judea that are in Christ. They only were hearing it said, "He who used to persecute us is now preaching the faith he once tried to destroy." And they glorified God because of me' (Galatians 1:21–24).

Luke recorded that after they saw the sails of his ship disappear on the horizon, 'the church throughout all Judea and Galilee and Samaria had peace and was being built up. And walking in the fear of the Lord and in the comfort of the Holy Spirit, it multiplied' (Acts 9:31).

Around this time, the church in Antioch was founded (Acts 11:19–21). Barnabas was sent there, and seeing the need for seasoned ministers in the church, left in search of Saul. Saul returned with him, and they served together as part of a team

---

[10] F.F. Bruce, *Paul – Apostle of the Free Spirit*, (Paternoster Press, Exeter, 1977), p.94

ministry. John Pollock commented that 'Antioch gave Paul home, friends and work to heal the scars and strains of the lonely decade now ended. It brought him back to the mainstream of the Christian church.'[11]

Antioch was the launch pad for Paul's missionary activity. Sent out with his friend Barnabas by the church leadership, he embarked on his first ministry tour. During that time, he reverted to his Roman name – Paul. Over the years to follow, he made at least another two missionary journeys. Most certainly Paul's ministry was incredibly fruitful. In the first instance, there were countless conversions to Christ. Both Jews and non-Jews (Gentiles) turned to Christ for salvation and experienced the life-changing dynamic of the Spirit of God within them.

F.F. Bruce wrote:

> ...as Paul persisted in preaching Jesus as the crucified Saviour and sin-bearer, the unexpected happened: pagans, as well as Jews and God-fearers, believed the message and found their lives transformed by a new, liberating power, which broke the stranglehold of selfishness and vice and purified them from within. The message of Christ crucified had thus accomplished something which no body of Greek philosophic teaching could have done for them.[12]

Paul also saw wonderful miracles. In fact, one cannot read the book of Acts and not notice this powerful dimension of the kingdom of God that characterised his life and ministry. Paul seemed to be surrounded by the miraculous – healings,

---

[11] John Pollock, *The Apostle*, (Hodder & Stoughton, London, 1969), p.45
[12] F.F. Bruce, *Paul – Apostle of the Free Spirit*, (Paternoster Press, Exeter, 1977), p.253

deliverances, earthquakes and even angelic interventions. To live with Paul was to live within the vicinity of the kingdom of God.

Mingled with all this was incredible suffering. Thomas Schreiner, in his magnificent book on Paul and his theology, wrote, 'Suffering was not a side effect of the Pauline mission; rather it was at the very centre of his apostolic evangelism. His distress validated and legitimated his message, demonstrating the truth of the gospel.'[13] We remember that when Paul sat in the house in Damascus, blinded, Jesus had sent a disciple called Ananias to pray for him. Ananias also had a prophetic word to be relayed to Saul: 'Go, for he is a chosen instrument of mine to carry my name before the Gentiles and kings and the children of Israel. For I will show him how much he must suffer for the sake of my name' (Acts 9:15,16).

Paul's life was truly extraordinary. F.F. Bruce said, 'He belongs to that select company who leave their mark on their time, who mould their contemporaries and exert an influence which stretches far into the future.'[14]

Then there were the letters that Paul wrote. These letters were full of teaching, establishing who Christ is, correcting errors, and motivating the believers to godly living. This was no occasional pastime, sharing a few nice thoughts with his friends; this was a strong, profound and integral part of his ministry. You cannot separate the life of Paul from the letters he wrote. They were so insightful and weighty that they are still having a life-changing effect on countless thousands of lives

---

[13] Thomas Schreiner, *Paul, Apostle of God's glory in Christ*, (IVP, Illinois, 2001), p.87
[14] F.F. Bruce, *Paul – Apostle of the Free Spirit*, (Paternoster Press, Exeter, 1977), p.462

today. Paul is long gone, but his letters live on. We are foolish if we ignore them.

Around half of them were penned within the confines of a prison cell. In fact, they can be divided into two categories: 'missionary' and 'captivity'. Some were written 'on the road' as it were, and some were written 'chained to a Roman soldier'. Wherever Paul found himself, neither his spirit nor his ministry were tethered.

How do we read the letters of Paul? In what light do we understand the things he wrote? Firstly, we must get into the heart and mind of the man who wrote them. What made Paul tick? The answer is that Paul was first and foremost an apostolic missionary, and it is in that light that we need to read his letters. This is the key to understanding all the theology and content of his letters. He did not write as a systematic theologian and a scholar, although he was one, having trained under one of the best in the land. Many people study his letters in that light and miss the heart of them.

He did not even write as a pastor. Although he visited the churches he planted, and knew many of the believers by name, Paul did not pastor these churches. He set up local leaderships for that role. If we study his letters purely through pastoral lenses, we will distort the heart of them. Paul wrote out of an apostolic anxiety. In his own words, '...apart from other things, there is the daily pressure on me of my anxiety for all the churches' (2 Corinthians 11:28). None of these churches were perfect. He wrote to instruct the new believers, challenge un-Christlike behaviour, correct immoral issues, disciple and guide the establishing of new leadership, and correct incoming heresies. We should avoid the romantic notion that the early church was perfect. Paul's letters were written to address its mess! During his ministry, Paul wrote 13 letters that we know of, from about AD 48 to 64 and likely many more.

Eventually Paul was arrested while visiting the temple at Jerusalem. He underwent several hearings and, after approximately two years of imprisonment, was shipped to Rome. It seems possible that after a hearing there, he was released and continued his ministry. At some point he was arrested again and sent to Rome for the second time. This time, the authorities found him guilty and beheaded him. It is believed that Peter, who was now also in Rome, was executed shortly afterwards by crucifixion (albeit upside down at his own request).

The New Testament Writings

The four Gospels are four accounts of the life of Jesus. It's widely accepted that Mark wrote the first Gospel after the execution of both Paul and Peter, at the request of the eldership in Rome, primarily for the Roman believers. Matthew, using Mark's framework, then penned a Gospel for the Jewish people, and Luke, using the same framework and his own extensive research, penned first his Gospel then the book of Acts. Luke wrote for a wide audience of both Jews and Gentiles. Years later, John wrote his Gospel, featuring many of the discourses of Jesus and specific miracles.

In our Bibles, the letters of Paul are followed by the anonymous letter to the Hebrews, and then by a letter from James, the half-brother of Jesus who was leading the church in Jerusalem. Following these, two letters from the apostle Peter, and then the astonishing three letters of John. There's also a small letter from Jude, another half-brother of Jesus.

Finally, the book of Revelation was written by John when exiled to the island of Patmos. In this book, John wrote of his encounter with Jesus, the glorified Lord of the churches, his profound glimpse into the life and worship of heaven, followed by a vision of the final downfall of Satan and triumph of Christ.

This vision foretells the fulfilling of a far greater vision. From before time began, God purposed something incredible for the sons and daughters of Adam. It was hinted at throughout the Old Testament and ushered in with the coming of Christ. Paul saw it clearly, and the church's mandate ever since has been to unfold and enact it, in preparation for its culmination at the end of time. The vision is of the church complete and glorified – the bride and body of Christ – comprised of people from every nation under the sun:

> After this I looked, and there was a great multitude that no one could count, from every nation, from all tribes and peoples and languages, standing before the throne and before the Lamb, robed in white, with palm branches in their hands. They cried out in a loud voice, saying, 'Salvation belongs to our God who is seated on the throne, and to the Lamb!' (Revelation 7:9, 10).

John's call to the church was fivefold.

Firstly, the church was to be a community of people learning to respond well to the love of God, giving time to express their love for Him in worship, learning the ways of Christ and His kingdom through the teaching of the Scriptures.

Secondly, they were to learn how to express the love of God to each other and to those in the communities around them. My friend Bob Duerden noted that, 'Again and again in the early centuries of the church, it was their commitment to providing for the poor and caring for the sick and dying that caused the authorities to begrudgingly acknowledge that they were good people.'

Thirdly, the church was to be a multinational community, growing and maturing in their knowledge and the mind of Christ. They were to harmonise their unique and different lives together into a oneness that would testify to the world around them that they all belonged to a single kingdom with its own remarkable culture and values. This often brought them into conflict with Jewish and local authorities, and especially with the Roman Empire. Many were martyred.

Fourthly, the church was to be missional in heart and outlook, telling others the good news of the kingdom. They were to realise the urgency of the gospel – that all people *needed* to find salvation in Christ. I think that over the exit doors of each church should be written these words: 'You are now entering your mission field.' I particularly like the mission statement of WEC (Worldwide Evangelisation Crusade): 'Our mission is to be crossing cultures to make disciples, starting churches where there are none or few, sharing the vision of the whole church, to the whole world and praying to see Jesus known, loved and worshipped.'[15] The founder of WEC, C.T. Studd,

---

[15] https://wec-uk.org/about

said, 'Some want to live within the sound of church or chapel bell; I want to run a rescue shop within a yard of hell.'[16]

Fifthly, the church was to be a community with their eyes and hopes in the future, living holy lives whilst waiting for Jesus' return. He won't come quietly to a borrowed manger the second time. It will be a triumphant 'full screen' appearance. The early church preached expecting that it would happen in their lifetime, but over time they realised that a thousand years is as one day with the Lord. They saw that the Lord Himself was patiently waiting for men and women everywhere to turn to Him in faith and repentance.

The Sequel to the Story

The story is not over, there is much still to come. At the end of His discourse on the signs of the end of the ages, Jesus said, 'Then will appear in heaven the sign of the Son of Man, and then all the tribes of the earth will mourn, and they will see the Son of Man coming on the clouds of heaven with power and great glory' (Matthew 24:30). To the disciples staring into the clouds where Jesus had been taken up, the angels said, 'Men of Galilee, why do you stand looking into heaven? This Jesus, who was taken up from you into heaven, will come in the same way as you saw him go' (Acts 1:11).

The apostle Paul in many places talks about the return of Christ. He wrote to the church in Thessalonica:

> ...for this we declare to you by a word from the Lord, that we who are alive, who are left until the coming of

---

[16] Norman Grubb, *C.T. Studd, Cricketer and Pioneer*, (Lutterworth Press, London, 1939), p.166

the Lord, will not precede those who have fallen asleep. For the Lord himself will descend from heaven with a cry of command, with the voice of an archangel, and with the sound of the trumpet of God. And the dead in Christ will rise first. Then we who are alive, who are left, will be caught up together with them in the clouds to meet the Lord in the air, and so we will always be with the Lord. Therefore encourage one another with these words (1 Thessalonians 4:15-18).

The apostle Peter saw it like this:

The Lord isn't really being slow about His promise, as some people think. No, He is being patient for your sake. He does not want anyone to be destroyed, but wants everyone to repent. But the day of the Lord will come as unexpectedly as a thief. Then the heavens will pass away with a terrible noise, and the very elements themselves will disappear in fire, and the earth and everything on it will be found to deserve judgment. Since everything around us is going to be destroyed like this, what holy and godly lives you should live, looking forward to the day of God and hurrying it along. On that day, He will set the heavens on fire, and the elements will melt away in the flames. But we are looking forward to the new heavens and new earth He has promised, a world filled with God's righteousness. And so, dear friends, while you are waiting for these things to happen, make every effort to be found living peaceful lives that are pure and blameless in His sight (2 Peter 3:9-14 - NLT).

What this new chapter of history will look like is only hinted at in the Scriptures. There is much we do not know, but we do understand that it will be unbelievably satisfying and beautiful. In the last book in the Narnia series, *The Last Battle*, C.S. Lewis described to the children what had happened at the end of time as they knew it. He wrote, 'The term is over: the holidays have begun. The dream is ended: this is the morning... now at last they were beginning Chapter One of the Great Story which no one on earth has read: which goes on for ever: in which every chapter is better than the one before.'[17]

In the previous three chapters, I have sought to paint a brushstroke sketch of biblical history. I could call it 'the big skim' because I have quickly scanned the surface of the huge narrative of God's people. However, there are many 'stopping places' along the way for those who want to pause and dig deeper. They will certainly find there are incredible insights to the activities of the triune God to be discovered.

In the next chapter, I want to start getting us into the Bible for ourselves. By now, our respect for the Bible should have grown, and our desire to plunge ourselves into the story of God intensified. So now we will turn our attention to how we read this Bible.

---

[17] C.S. Lewis, *The Last Battle*, (Grafton, London, 2002), pp.171,172

Chapter 6

The Approach to the Bible

The approach distance for an aircraft to land at London's Heathrow airport is about 15 miles. It does not suddenly drop out of the sky onto the runway! In a similar way, our approach to the Bible will take some time for it to be truly effective and fruitful. This is not a book to be hurried. It holds something divine, and that needs to be both recognised and honoured.

The World within the Words

The Bible we hold in our hands contains the living Word within the written word. Somehow, in these words on the pages of your Bible, are the spoken and living words of God, and they still speak to us. We do not read dead text. The writer to the Hebrews wrote, 'For the word of God is *living and active*, sharper than any two-edged sword, piercing to the division of soul and of spirit, of joints and of marrow, and discerning the thoughts and intentions of the heart' (Hebrews 4:12; emphasis mine). The apostle Peter wrote of '...the *living and abiding* word of God...' (1 Peter 1:23; emphasis mine). This is the first thing to be aware of as we handle God's book. **It contains a life of its own.**

The second thing we need to be aware of is that these are words, not so much to be read, **but to be heard**. God speaks through the words of the Bible, and therefore we must learn to hear the voice of the Lord as we read and meditate on the Scriptures. We must also note the difference between the *logos* (written) word and the *rhema* (spoken) word. The former informs; the latter transforms. We must not come to this book purely for spiritual information, but also, and may I say primarily, for spiritual transformation. The Bible is specifically designed to bring about deep changes in our lives.

The third thing to be aware of is that the Bible **reveals the things of God**. Remember the illustration of the wardrobe in *The Lion, the Witch and the Wardrobe*? As we press into reading, studying and meditating in this book, we will find ourselves entering into another world that is far more powerful than the one we live in. In my experience, the further I press into the world of the Bible, the more I sense the wind blowing from another land.

Years ago, I wrote in the flyleaf of my Bible these words: 'The conductor looks at the score and hears the symphony. I muse in the Book and I hear the music of heaven, the conversations around the throne, and I sense the movements of the Almighty.' As we delve deeply into the pages of the Scriptures, we will find ourselves drawn into encounters with God the Father, Jesus the Son and the Holy Spirit. We will become more and more aware of the values and movements of the kingdom of heaven.

It is here that we enter the realms of faith. The Bible says that 'without faith it is impossible to please Him, for whoever would draw near to God must believe that He exists and that He rewards those who seek Him' (Hebrews 11:6). When we approach the Scriptures, we need to believe that God wants to speak to us. The Scriptures are not simply an account of what happened thousands of years ago, they are the means by which the living God still communicates to us.

I was part of a missionary church planting team in France back in the early 70s. I was also engaged to Mo. She was studying at a teacher training college in Portsmouth. For two years we hardly saw each other. The internet had not been invented, and neither had mobile phones! We managed to have one phone call each year from the local Post Office. But we wrote scores of letters to each other. (We still have them in shoe boxes in our loft!) As we read each other's thoughts written on paper, we began to understand each other. The more we read, the more we knew. Our letters became our conversation. In the same way, the Bible is God's living letter to us, full of His words, thoughts, ways of doing things and His truth. The more we prayerfully and carefully read it, listening for His voice, the more we enter into conversation with Him, getting to know Him.

Setting the Scene

The theology of most people today has been developed around the sermons they have heard, the songs they sing, the books they have read and are reading, and anecdotes found on social media. It is unfortunately rare to find someone whose understanding of the triune God and His ways has come primarily through a sustained, systematic absorbing of the Scriptures.

Here's a thought: Bible conferences and large events can be likened to huge spiritual restaurants where people go occasionally for a really good meal. A Sunday sermon is like going out for lunch, where someone else has done all the preparation and serves the meal. Daily snippets of God from the various Bible notes booklets that are available can be compared to a quick ready-made snack to keep us going. However good these all are, they cannot compare to a regular diet.

Part of the process of growing up is learning to prepare our own meals. Instead of having others feed us, or living off 'tinned' spiritual food, we should learn to prepare our own spiritual meals, feeding ourselves on a regular basis.

Spiritual Preparation

In this section, I want to lay some groundwork for the effective reading of the Bible. To get the most out of the Scriptures we must think long term. Spiritual maturity is not a gift that can be imparted but a fruit that needs to be nurtured. **We therefore have need of patient perseverance**. We live today in an age of the immediate, where long-term thinking and even planning is alien to a lot of people. We are easily bored, and we are told that our attention spans are shrinking. We need to challenge this and realise that spiritual maturity is not a gift that can be conferred in a moment of prayer, but rather, that it comes through months and years of consistent walking with God.

We also live in an age of speed reading. We skim to get the gist of what is being communicated through the printed books or the overload of information through social media. Through wanting to grasp much, we absorb nothing of value.

When we hear breathtaking brilliance from musicians, it may sound spontaneous, but behind it is daily, repetitive – often boring – rehearsals, exercises and training. In 1987, I watched a Southbank show featuring Melvyn Bragg interviewing Eric Clapton, noted for his long guitar solos. (He still happens to be my favourite guitarist.) Towards the end of the programme, the conversation went like this:

> Melvyn: So what goes through your mind as you are about to start a solo?
>
> Eric: For me, I just start singing... but I do it with the guitar.[1]

When I heard that, I had to stop and think through what Eric had just revealed about his guitar playing. What he sang in his head was instantly transferred to the fretboard of his instrument, and not just the notes but every nuance. It occurred to me that here was a man who intimately knew the fretboard of his guitar. He had worked with it systematically through years of practice. Scales had been memorised, and he and his guitar had become almost one. What he sang in his head was played instantaneously on his guitar.

Eric is a highly skilled blues guitarist. Now here's an interesting thing: In the Old Testament, the young David was known as being skilled on the harp (1 Samuel 16:16–18). The Hebrew word used is *yâda*, and it basically means 'to know intimately'. Eric Clapton is skilled because he 'knows' the fretboard on his guitar like the back of his hand. But there is

---

[1] https://www.youtube.com/watch?v=OpORGik_cug

also a deep sense of love involved in this word. Eric's drive to master his craft is fuelled by a love of the blues. Love will take us much further than simply learning. Love loves to learn.

How then did Eric arrive at that level of skill? The answer is simple: practice, practice, practice. We all love to see brilliant performances on the stages and the sports fields but, as Dallas Willard pointed out, 'The star performer himself didn't achieve his excellence by trying to behave in a certain way only during the game. Instead he chose an overall life of preparation of mind and body, pouring all his energies into that total preparation, to provide a foundation in the body's automatic responses and strength for his conscious efforts during the game. ...it is a daily regimen that no one sees.'[2]

One of my favourite characters from the Old Testament is Ezra. 'He was a scribe skilled in the Law of Moses that the LORD, the God of Israel, had given...' (Ezra 7:6). The Hebrew word for 'skilled' here is *mâhir*, meaning 'quick, diligent, prompt'. It's rooted in the word *mâhar*, which means 'flowing easily.' It is also written that '...Ezra had set his heart to study the Law of the LORD, and to do it and to teach his statutes and rules in Israel' (Ezra 7:10). Notice the order: study, do, teach.

When we think of practice, or personal discipline, there are three important words for us to get hold of. The first important one is **discipleship**. The word 'disciple' is the English translation of the Greek word *mathētēs* and, in the truest sense of the word, it means 'an apprentice, a student, a pupil.' Such an individual puts their learning under the direction of a master –

---

[2] Dallas Willard, *The Spirit of the Disciplines*, (Harper & Row, San Francisco, 1988), pp.3,4

accompanying, listening, watching and applying what is learnt. A disciple, therefore, is someone with a teachable spirit who is willing to listen, learn, and put what has been learned into practice.

The word 'disciple' also carries the idea of a disciplined lifestyle. This is what Paul meant when he told Timothy to 'train yourself for godliness, for while bodily training is of some value, godliness is of value in every way, as it holds promise for the present life and also for the life to come' (1 Timothy 4:7,8). The word 'train' is from the Greek word *gumnazo*, from which we get our word gymnasium. People go to the gym to get fit. Gordon MacDonald wrote, 'If we are ever to develop a spiritual life that gives contentment, it will be because we approach spiritual living as a discipline, much as an athlete trains his body for competition.'[3]

Here, then, we see the idea of a spiritual athlete. Antony of Egypt, the founder of the Desert Fathers, said that the followers of Christ were the *athletae Dei*, the 'athletes of God', with a single-hearted devotion to the goal of Christlikeness. For Antony, spiritual exercises were to train the body and the soul in righteousness. This in turn, produced highly disciplined men and women who could run a long race, standing firm and battling through when life gets really tough. The apostle Paul's testimony toward the end of his life was 'I have fought the good fight, I have finished the race, I have kept the faith' (2 Timothy 4:7).

---

[3] Gordon MacDonald, *Ordering Your Private World*, (Moody Press, Nashville, 1985), p.117

The second important word is **asceticism**. The Greek word *askesis*. We get our word 'ascetic' from it. However, the word 'ascetic' has been ruined over the years. Today it conjures up thoughts of being 'emaciated, harsh, haters of pleasure, strictly religious'. The Oxford Dictionary says that it speaks of 'a person who practises severe self-discipline and abstains from all forms of pleasure.'[4]

Yet originally, it was to do with training for excellence 'backed up by years of repetitive behaviours that are the very antithesis of spontaneity.'[5] The apostle Paul wrote, 'Do you not know that in a race all the runners run, but only one receives the prize? So run that you may obtain it. Every athlete exercises self-control in all things. They do it to receive a perishable wreath, but we an imperishable. So I do not run aimlessly; I do not box as one beating the air. But I discipline my body and keep it under control, lest after preaching to others I myself should be disqualified' (1 Corinthians 9:24–27).

Paul mentioned here running, but aimlessly, with no direction; he discussed boxing, but with no target. He was talking about pointless expenditures of energy. However, when it comes to his own life, he disciplined himself, seeing his undisciplined self as an enemy to the purposes of God, and as an enemy to conquer and subdue. He feared being disqualified. The last thing he wanted was to stand before the Lord and have the Lord say, 'All I saw from your life was bluster and noise, but you have constructed nothing of value.'

---

[4] *The Oxford Dictionary, ascetic*, (Clarendon Press, Oxford, 1990), p.62
[5] Eugene Peterson, *Working the Angles*, (Eerdmans, Michigan, 1987), p.14

True asceticism involves developing the ability to refuse our personal impulses and whims. None of these have substantial capabilities in directing our lives correctly.

This brings me to the third important word, which is **renunciation.** *The Bloomsbury Dictionary* describes the word as meaning 'a denial or rejection of something or somebody, usually for moral or religious reasons.'[6] This is perfectly biblical. The writer to the Hebrews exhorted the believers, 'let us also lay aside every weight, and sin which clings so closely...' (Hebrews 12:1). He used the Greek word *apothemenoi*, which meant 'to put off or aside or away'. If we are serious about following hard after the Lord, then there will be some relationships, some things, some mindsets and even attitudes that we will have to firmly relinquish.

If we are going to pursue excellence in any career or vocation, we must purposefully develop an ongoing practice of renunciation, carefully removing those things that would hinder our progress. Jesus talked about pruning a fruitful vine in order that it may bear more fruit. John recorded His words. 'Every branch in me that does not bear fruit he takes away, *and every branch that does bear fruit he prunes, that it may bear more fruit*' (John 15:2 – emphasis mine). Paul wrote in two places in his letter to the church in Corinth, "All things are lawful for me," *but not all things are helpful.* "All things are lawful for me," *but I will not be dominated by anything*' (1 Corinthians 6:12 – emphasis mine). This refrain is echoed later in 1 Corinthians 10:23, with the reply '*But not all things build up*' (emphasis

---

[6] *The Bloomsbury Dictionary, renunciation,* (Bloomsbury Publishing Plc, London, 2004), p.1580

mine). The pursuit of a deep and meaningful spirituality needs to be ordered by simplicity, and that involves deliberately removing the superfluous from our lives, however painful it seems at first. Renunciation is a big word, but it is not a difficult word for lovers of God. The disciplined life, the ascetic life and the life of renunciation is not a grim and onerous life. To be honest, when we are deeply attracted to God and His ways, the things of this earth that we once thought necessary, will begin to lose their allure. In any relationship, sacrifice is easy when one is deeply and truly in love.

Authentic renunciation sets us free to focus. Monica Furlong, writing in her biography of the Cistercian monk Thomas Merton, observed that the rigours of the Trappist/Cistercian monastery at Gethsemani in Kentucky were specifically designed 'that monks should be set free from other distractions and therefore able to concentrate on the contemplation of God.'[7] Asceticism and renunciation focus our attention on the important things.

We need to develop a personal askesis. To use another analogy, it is like the cultivating of a garden, driving down deep roots into the life of God. To build a strong house you must also dig deep. Jesus said, 'everyone who comes to me and hears my words and does them, I will show you what he is like: he is like a man building a house, who dug deep and laid the foundation on the rock. And when a flood arose, the stream broke against that house and could not shake it, because it had been well built' (Luke 6:47–49). To build strong, you must dig deep. Bear this in mind – roots and foundations are not seen, but they are

---

[7] Monica Furlong, *Merton: A Biography*, (SPCK, London, 1995), p.112

essential. Digging down into God is a private activity for God's eyes only. God sees the roots; others will eventually see the fruits.

Everybody wants to see the fruits of spirituality. Yet the man or woman who is serious with God will not concentrate primarily on the fruit, but on developing strong, deep roots of spirituality. Today's culture is often 'results driven', whereas the culture of the kingdom of heaven lies in the cultivation of character and values. If the life is right, the fruit grows quite naturally – it does not have to be forced.

These words, *discipline, askesis* and *renunciation* must not become negative concepts in our thinking; they are spiritual disciplines that put us in a good position to sense and hear God more clearly. They are like spiritual frameworks and, believe me, God is not frightened by frameworks. The fact that our body stands upright, and can move, is because of the firm skeletal framework that it is built around and upon, which holds it all in place.

Yet, I must stress, it is all about relationship – about knowing the Lord. Any serving that we do, and any ministry that we exercise, must come *out of* this relationship. Let me explain. The Lord first made Himself known to me in 1969. Since then, I have done mission work, pastored churches, served on various teams and elderships, mentored people, and preached and taught the Bible. Much of my thinking and discussion and activity has been around 'the King's business'. I now know the 'business' of the kingdom quite well and yet, in the centre of my being, there has always been a yearning. I have carried this overwhelming sense that, although all this other stuff is important, the most important thing to Jesus is that He wants me to walk with Him and know Him. Throughout the busyness of my days there has always been a calling from Him, from which I cannot – nor do I desire to – escape. It is to be intimate with Him.

I once felt rebuked by the Lord when He said to me, 'You have more of a relationship with your diary than you have with me.' It is so easy to fall into the trap of thinking that a full diary is what God wants from us. I had to learn that an overactive ministry is seriously detrimental to a healthy inner life. Eugene Peterson once asked the rhetorical question, 'How can I lead people into the quiet place beside the still waters if I am in perpetual motion?'[8]

God will not align Himself to our pace of life. We must learn to align ourselves to Him – to take time to stop, to think, to reflect and to become. If you and I want to know Him, we must give Him time.

There is a famous story in the Gospel of Luke about two sisters. Jesus had been invited to eat with them. One of the sisters, Martha, set herself to preparing a meal, whilst her other sister, seeing that Jesus was teaching, sat at His feet listening to Him. After a while, Martha became upset and exasperated with her sister who, in her eyes, was shirking. She walked over to Jesus and vented her anger. Jesus, instead of backing her up, gently reprimanded her for being so wrapped up in what she was doing *for* Him. He told her that her service, as good as it was, was distracting her from Him (Luke 10:38–42).

---

[8] Eugene Peterson, *The Contemplative Pastor*, (Eerdmans, Michigan, 1989), p.19

I have this overarching impression that the Lord looks, not so much for what we do for Him, but for our friendship and companionship with Him. This is to be the priority of our lives, out of which all else will flow.

Although we should be in for the long haul, so many want short cuts. Many want quick snatches of the biblical story, and some have even developed the posture of tourists in the kingdom of heaven. They wander through the sites taking snapshots. They gather spiritual experiences as trinkets. True spiritual directors are not tour guides but instructors and trainers in 'long haul living' with Christ in this world. They will teach you not to look at what has been excavated by others, but how to dig for yourself.

Making time and finding a place is integral to developing a close walk with Jesus. To develop a close walk with God, cultivating an intimate dialogue with Him through word and prayer will mean that we need to commit to the following practices:

Find and Maintain a Regular Time

It is true that we can meet with God whenever we want to, but my own research and experience has shown me that the best time is in the morning, usually before all else starts. For some, this is very difficult, especially mothers of young children! In their case, time must often be snatched, asking the Lord to create some sacred space during their frenetic day.

This is where personal discipline really kicks in. If we are to take our time with the Lord seriously, then we should consider not only the time we get up, but also the time we go to bed. The Scripture is clear: 'It is in vain that you rise up early and go late to rest, eating the bread of anxious toil; for he gives to his beloved sleep' (Psalm 127:2). Many a godly Christian has guarded both aspects of the day. On a personal note, I often clear my desk in the evening, and lay out my Bible ready for the morning. I have learned to anticipate the morning encounter with God.

The Hebrew understanding of a day is that it starts in the evening. The book of Genesis says repeatedly, 'and there was evening and there was morning, the first day' (Genesis 1:3, 8, 13, 19, 23, 31). This is how it works: while we sleep, God is already at work, and so we awake refreshed into a world that we didn't make, and into scenarios in which He has already been actively at work if only we have eyes to see. Upon waking, we are attentive to the planning and strategies of God. We hear His voice, feeding and nourishing our souls. In my view, it is better, and more biblical, to spend time with God in the morning, 'mapping it out' with Him, rather than 'mopping it up' with Him before going to bed.

In the book of Exodus, God provided the people with manna from heaven. It arrived first thing in the morning, and the Scripture says, 'Morning by morning they gathered it, each as much as he could eat; but when the sun grew hot, it melted' (Exodus 16:21). Two more things on this. What was gathered on Monday was of no use for Tuesday; they had to gather every day (except the Sabbath). Also, they had to get up to gather it. There was no angel gently tugging the flaps of the tent with a home delivery!

Many of the great biblical characters were early risers. (See Genesis 19:27; 28:18 / Exodus 24:4; 34:4 / Joshua 3:1; 7:16 /

Psalm 119:147, 148 / Isaiah 50:4 / Mark 1:35) Have a look at these Scriptures before you move on. The phrase 'early in the morning' is found 36 times in the Bible.

In the book of Jeremiah, we also find some interesting Scriptures. For example, God rebukes those who came to worship at the temple, 'when I spoke to you persistently you did not listen, and when I called you, you did not answer' (Jeremiah 7:13). However, in the NASB it reads, 'I spoke to you, *rising up early and speaking*, but you did not hear, and I called you and you did not answer...' (emphasis mine). Jeremiah used the Hebrew word *shâkam*, which meant 'to rise or start early, to make an early start.' It also carries the sense of persistence. The overall sense is that God had something to say, and He started early to demonstrate the importance of what He wanted to say, and it was a word that lingered through the day. This expression is repeated in Jeremiah 11: 25, where we read, 'Since the day that your fathers came out of the land of Egypt until this day, I have sent you all My servants the prophets, daily rising and sending them...' Compare these verses with 11:7, where it says that God was 'rising early and warning...' and in 25:3,4, the prophet had spoken to the people of God, 'rising early and speaking...' and that the Lord had sent all His prophets 'rising early and sending...'

Robert Murray M'Cheyne was a Scottish minister who died of typhus at the young age of 29 in 1843. It was said of him that his 'brief ministry of seven-and-a-half years had stamped an indelible impress on Scotland.'[9] He loved to rise early to spend time with God, and in his journal, on the Sunday morning

---

[9] Andrew Bonar, *Robert Murray M'Cheyne*, (Banner of Truth, Edinburgh, 1972), p.3

of the 23 February 1834, he wrote these words: 'Sabbath – Rose early to seek God, and found him whom my soul loveth. Who would not rise early to meet such company?'[10] These words made a huge impact on my own life.

One way to start is to determine a time, maybe 20 minutes at first. Get up a little earlier, make a cup of tea or coffee, and then sit with the Scriptures in front of you, asking God to speak to you. Stay with this routine for at least a month. Two things will happen: firstly, you will have developed a habit, and secondly, the 20 minutes will not feel long enough.

Find and Maintain a Secret Place

Jesus said, 'When you pray, go into your room and shut the door and pray to your Father who is in secret. And your Father who sees in secret will reward you' (Matt. 6:6). The secret place or the hidden place is where true spirituality is most deeply nurtured. The results of that nurturing are then authenticated and honed in community. But firstly, it is found and nourished in the quietness of a secret walk and conversation with God. In this all the spiritual masters are agreed. Thomas à Kempis, in his incredible book *The Imitation of Christ*, wrote a whole chapter entitled 'The love of solitude and silence'. In it he says, 'Anyone, then, who aims to live the inner and spiritual life must go apart, with Jesus, from the crowd.'[11]

There is a difference between loneliness and solitude. One is imposed whilst the other is chosen. One is inner emptiness, the other is inner fulfilment. I do not choose solitude to escape, rather I choose it to replenish myself with God.

---

[10] Ibid, p.30
[11] Thomas à Kempis, *The Imitation of Christ*, (Hendrickson, Massachusetts, 2004), p.20

In the Old Testament, there are references to specific places where the Lord said that He would meet with His people. One place was at the ark in the tabernacle, between the two cherubim. God said to Moses, 'There I will meet with you' (Exodus 25:22). Another was the entrance to the tabernacle. God said, 'I will meet with you, to speak with you there...' (Exodus 29:42), adding, 'there I will meet with the people of Israel...' (Exodus 29:43). In the book of Numbers, God spoke to Moses of 'the tent of meeting before the testimony, where I meet with you' (Numbers 17:4). Later, God's meeting place would be in Solomon's temple.

Nevertheless, there were times when God met with people where they were. He was not restricted to a place made with human hands. In the New Testament, we find the temple was no longer to be considered as a meeting place. Instead, God would reside in human hearts. Paul wrote to the corporate church at Corinth, 'Do you not know that you are God's temple and that God's Spirit dwells in you?' (1 Corinthians 3:16.) Church is the arena where we gather to experience the presence and fragrant power of His kingdom.

Paul also wrote to the individual believers in Corinth, '...do you not know that your body is a temple of the Holy Spirit within you, whom you have from God?' (1 Corinthians 6:19). This is frankly astonishing! Paul was teaching that the Holy Spirit, the manifest presence of God, had taken up residence in the lives of each individual believer. In the same way, we who believe are housing the presence of the God who created the heavens and the earth.

Somewhere, in the middle of these two concepts of a physical place and a non-physical place is what Spiritual Theology calls 'a thin place'. The first time I heard this expression I was watching a television programme featuring the Christian band *Iona* playing on the island of Lindisfarne, or 'Holy Island' in 1995. During the programme there was an interview with a Christian dancer called Andy Raine. He was asked by the presenter, 'Why do people make a pilgrimage to this island?' Andy replied that it was because the island is 'a thin place', and explained that concept by saying that, for hundreds of years, people had prayed and worshipped God here, and the veil between heaven and earth, in this particular place, was gossamer thin. You could almost immediately sense His presence as you stepped on this island, hallowed by holy activity. Constant holy activity had left a holy residue.

Many years ago, I went to Westminster Chapel. I knew something of the history of the place. Dr G. Campbell Morgan, followed by Dr Martyn Lloyd-Jones, had been the previous ministers there. Both men had exercised a strong and fruitful preaching ministry. At that time, Dr R.T. Kendall was the minister, and he, too, was an outstanding preacher. As I was looking around the sanctuary, I looked up at the famous pulpit where these two giants of faith had preached. I then spoke to Louise, Dr Kendall's wife, who happened to be in the church sanctuary. I asked her if I could climb up to the pulpit, and she readily agreed. As I entered the pulpit, noticing the leather chair and the well-worn pulpit desk, and realising that the only activity that had ever taken place here over decades was the anointed preaching of the Word of God. I felt the holy residue. It was a thin place.

Conversely, in the days when charismatic churches met in village halls and other local venues, often they felt the need to pray about the atmosphere of the place when they turned up on a Sunday morning to set up for the meeting. There was often a darker residue hanging in the air.

So, what am I saying? Simply this – find yourself a place where you can be alone with God each day. As you make it a holy habit of meeting Him there each day, after a while the place will become a thin place, and it will have its own drawing power.

Find and Develop an Attitude

As we make time to be alone with God, we need to develop an attitude of reverence. One Scripture that has deeply affected how I approach God is found in the book of Ecclesiastes. Solomon wrote, 'Guard your steps when you go to the house of God. To draw near to listen is better than to offer the sacrifice of fools, for they do not know that they are doing evil. Be not rash with your mouth, nor let your heart be hasty to utter a word before God, for God is in heaven and you are on earth. Therefore let your words be few' (Ecclesiastes 5:1,2). To be silent before God, not rushing in with a long list of requirements, shows respect. We enter this thin place with a 'shhhh' in our spirit. David wrote, 'For God alone my soul waits in silence; from Him comes my salvation.... For God alone, my soul, wait in silence' (Psalm 62:1,5).

The Trinity Annual Conference released a 'DIY retreat' paper during the Covid-19 pandemic. Concerning the creating of a space to be alone with God, it said, 'In solitude, we seek a full turning to God who is in us and with us. We focus on him, we turn our minds, hearts towards him. We unplug or detach ourselves from everything that distracts us from being present with God. This includes our handphones, tablets, laptops, social media, and even people, that we have become dependent on and can distract us. Solitude gives us time and space to explore and know ourselves in God's presence.'[12] The paper continued by saying, 'Come into God's presence, slow down, relax and intentionally release the chaos, tension and noise in your mind to him.'[13]

How we come to this book is vitally important. We should come with a sense of respect. David wrote, 'my heart stands in awe of your words' (Psalm 119:161). We should also come willing to be taught. We do not look to the Bible to reinforce what we believe, but rather to change what we believe. This book will enable us to change the way we think, feel, act and react. We will want to come under the guidance of the Holy Spirit. Jesus told the disciples, 'He will guide you into all the truth' (John 16:13). The Holy Spirit will take us into the world of the Scriptures, opening truths up before our eyes, revealing to us the heart of the Father and teaching us the ways of Christ. Take some time to consider 1 Corinthians 2:9–14. This passage talks about the ministry of the Holy Spirit, who 'searches everything, even the depths of God'. The Spirit, who loves to explore the depths of God, lives in us. I conclude, therefore, that all Christians should be explorers of God!

---

[12] TRAC Institute for Christian Ministry Resources 2020, http://www.trac.org.my/view_file.cfm?fileid=357.
[13] Ibid.

We begin our time in the Bible with prayer. Remember this is the Word of God, not a dead book. Time spent with the Word should be time spent in conversation with The Word, Jesus. There are three things we could pray: the first is that the Lord would **open our eyes**. David wrote, 'Open my eyes that I may behold wondrous things out of your law' (Psalm 119:18). The second is that the Lord would **open our mind** to understand the Scriptures. Luke records that Jesus, when He was with the disciples after His Resurrection, said to them, '"These are my words that I spoke to you while I was still with you, that everything written about me in the Law of Moses and the Prophets and the Psalms must be fulfilled." Then he opened their minds to understand the Scriptures...' (Luke 24:44,45). The third is that the Lord would **open our ears** to hear His voice. The prophet Isaiah wrote, 'Morning by morning he awakens; he awakens my ear to hear as those who are taught. The Lord God has opened my ear, and I was not rebellious; I turned not backward' (Isaiah 50:4,5). David also prayed, 'In sacrifice and offering you have not delighted, but you have given me an open ear. Burnt offering and sin offering you have not required' (Psalm 40:6).

In this chapter, we have thought about our approach to the Bible. We have considered the importance of prioritising building a relationship with God through this book. We have realised the necessity of establishing personal disciplines to facilitate this. Now, we are ready to start.

CHAPTER 7

STARTING TO READ THE BIBLE

Over the years that I have been reading the Bible, I have been greatly helped by many theologians who were also lovers of the Scriptures. Among them are J.I. Packer, Eugene Peterson, Michael Casey, to name a few. All their books are worth getting and keeping.

I like what Eugene Peterson wrote about reading the Bible. He said, 'Christian spirituality is, in its entirety, rooted in and shaped by the scriptural text.'[1] He added, 'Christians feed on Scripture. Holy Scripture nurtures the holy community as food nurtures the human body.'[2]

William of St Thierry was a Cistercian monk living in the 12th century. He wrote:

> The Scriptures need to be read and understood in the same spirit in which they were written. You will never enter into Paul's meaning until by constant application

---
[1] Eugene Peterson, *Eat this book*, (Hodder & Stoughton, London, 2006), p.15
[2] Ibid, p.18

to reading him and giving yourself to meditation you have imbibed his spirit. You will never understand David, unless by experience you have made the very sentiments of the psalms your own. And that applies to all Scripture. There is the same gulf between attentive study and mere reading as there is between friendship and acquaintance with a passing guest, between boon companionship and chance meeting.[3]

Your Bible

The first thing I would recommend is that you get yourself a good version of the Bible. For those beginning the journey into the biblical world, I would suggest either the New Living Translation or the New International Version. They are quite accurate and are easy to read. For those who want to get more serious, I would recommend the English Standard Version or the New American Standard Bible. These are very literal translations.

At this point, I would say that digital versions are helpful for quick referencing, but not for serious study. My friend Bob Duerden pointed out that 'having a printed Bible also enables you to get a much better sense of how the different books fit together in the overall scheme of the Scriptures.' I agree.

I suggest that you get yourself a Bible with a good size print. Hopefully, you are going to be perusing its pages often, and therefore you don't want to put undue pressure on your eyes!

Be prepared to spend some money on it, because it is going to become a good friend to you for years to come. We wouldn't

---

[3] https://www.stanbrookabbey.org.uk/who-we-are/a-day-in-the-life/lexio-divina/

think twice of spending money on a good pair of shoes before a long hike. Invest in a good Bible that is going to last you for years.

When it comes to reading it, position yourself comfortably, preferably at a table. I have a little reading stand that I place my Bible on so that my back is in a good position. On occasions, I sit in an armchair with my Bible nestling on a couple of cushions on my lap.

For the sake of your eyes, make sure that you have good lighting. I remember years ago some advice from my optician, who was also a Christian. He told me that reading in an office with strip lighting is the worst way to read any kind of book. He said that the best light is a desk lamp with the light directly over the pages. If, however, you prefer sitting in a chair, an over the shoulder lamp should work.

Where do I Start?

In the late 60s, when I became a Christian, I was given my first Bible by a man called John Smale, the father of my good friend, Ishmael. I opened it at the beginning, as we all normally do with a book, and started reading. Some of it was great and some of it was heavy going, especially for someone like me who had no idea what the Bible was all about! Nevertheless, I persevered and ploughed my way through.

Then I met Ralph, one of my first mentors. I mentioned him in chapter one. We were having a conversation about reading the Bible and he asked me how I did it. I told him about reading it from the beginning to the end, and that when I got to books like Leviticus and Deuteronomy, I found it heavy going. He looked at me with a smile on his face and said, 'Alan, you are having a lot of meat and potatoes in your spiritual diet. You need also a daily dose of vitamins.' He then explained that I needed to introduce into my reading portions from both the Old and the New Testaments. I put that into practice and the heavy going got a lot easier!

Since that time, I have developed a system of reading the Bible that has proved so beneficial to me. It is a method that I have now taught for decades. I call it 'The Five Finger Method.'

Finger One – Continuous Reading

Using the analogy of the hand, the first finger is continuous reading. We need to read the Bible methodically, systematically, thoroughly and deeply. This is where we learn to go through the whole Bible, whole books, whole gospels and whole letters. This way we get the bigger picture. A.T. Pierson, in his biography of George Müller, wrote, 'Continuous reading of the Word will in due course throw light upon the general teaching of the Word, revealing God's thoughts in their variety and connection, and will go far to correct erroneous views.'[4]

There are those who skip about in their reading of Scripture, having favourite texts or passages that they often refer to. I understand that, but we do need to dig into unfamiliar areas. It is the difference between listening to our favourite albums or playlists, where you know what is coming next, and listening to the radio or someone else's playlist, where you don't know.

When replying to a group of Sadducees who had come to trip Him up in His teaching, Jesus said, 'You are wrong, because

---

[4] A.T. Pierson, *George Müller of Bristol*, (Pantianos Classics, first published 1899), pp.168,169

you know neither the Scriptures nor the power of God' (Matthew 22:29). The best antidote to error is a thorough knowledge of the truth. On occasions, I have asked a congregation the question: 'How many of you have read the Bible from cover to cover?' I have watched a few hands go up, and usually it is about five percent of the people sitting in front of me.

I certainly do not recommend the 'skip about' method. This type of reading produces nothing but well-worn sections of the Bible. It would do us good to challenge ourselves with the thought that a Muslim boy in Saudi Arabia, for example, will have both read and memorised the whole of the Qur'an by the time he is 14 years old. I have rarely met someone of that age who had read the whole of the New Testament.

Neither do I recommend the 'open up and point' method. This is where we ask the Lord for a Scripture to help us, then randomly open the Bible and point to a text. This methodology can really lead you up the garden path. The story is told of a man who, looking for guidance, opened his Bible and rested his finger on Matthew 27:5. Unhappy with what he read he repeated the process and pointed at Luke 10:37. Still unhappy, he did it again and came to John 13:27. Have a look at them and then draw your own conclusions!

I do recommend that we develop a regular reading pattern. For an absolute beginner, I suggest starting with the Gospel of Mark, reading it right through several times. Mark was the first to write an account of the life and death of Jesus and it reads very easily. After that, read through all four Gospels several times. Then read the whole of the New Testament several times, whilst starting to go slowly through Psalms and Proverbs. Once you have done that, I recommend the following pattern of reading to give us a truly balanced diet. It is a pattern that I have developed and adopted over the years.

Firstly, there is my *devotional* reading. I say that, because these are the eight books where I look to encounter the heart and mind of the Lord, seeking to deepen my relationship with Him. If I am honest, much of my theology has arisen from the slow, meditative reading of these books. I start with Psalm 1, and then the next day I read Psalm 2. Then, over several weeks, I read a psalm each day. (When it comes to Psalm 119, I take about a week with it, reading three or four sections at a time. They are helpfully divided into the Hebrew alphabetical order.) When I have finished the book of Psalms, I turn my attention to the Gospel of Matthew, reading one chapter daily. 28 days later, when I have finished the book, I go to the book of Proverbs, reading one chapter daily. 32 days later, I start the Gospel of Mark, followed by Ecclesiastes, followed by the Gospel of Luke, followed by the Song of Solomon, ending with the Gospel of John. On each, I read a chapter a day.

It looks like this:

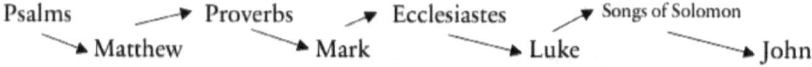

Secondly, I start on my *vitamin* reading. Here I begin with the Acts of the Apostles, and then work my way through all the letters of Paul, and the others, ending with the book of Revelation. Again, I seek to read one chapter a day. I miss out the four gospels because I am already covering them in my devotional reading.

Thirdly, I get into my *meat and potatoes* reading. I make a start with the book of Genesis, and work my way through, seeking to do three chapters a day. I read right through to the book of Malachi, missing out Psalms, Proverbs, Ecclesiastes, and the Song of Solomon because I am already covering them. In all, I seek to read around five chapters a day.

Having said that, please do not get hung up on the five chapters a day. That is just a rough guide. You may do considerably less one day if you come across a verse or passage that grabs your attention, inviting you to think about it and respond to it. Another day, you may read considerably more, either because you have got a lot of time on your hands, or you have got caught up in the flow of a story.

Using this approach will help you to know where you are going and to check where you are up to. Having said that, keeping to the scheme will easily get you through the whole Bible in a year.

Here is a thought for you: Robert Chapman, a contemporary of George Müller, and a devout and careful reader of the Bible, wrote, 'A careless reader of Scripture never made a close walker with God.'[5]

Let me quote at large Ralph Shallis, the man who first instilled in me a disciplined love for the Scriptures. He wrote of his own experience:

> At first, I found all this discipline pretty tough going. But after a few months, it ceased to be hard: it became an unspeakable joy. God began to reveal himself to my soul in a way that no words can describe...

---

[5] Robert Cleaver Chapman, *Choice sayings*, (Scholar's Choice, United States, 2015)

> After I read the Bible through several times, I began to discover a positive pattern in God's thought, a sequence in his revelation. I could now follow the development of his purpose from the beginning until his final issue at the end of time...
>
> I was discovering a new universe, the kingdom of God itself. [6]

Finger Two – Verse or Passage Study

Often when I take a walk around the lakes at the back of our house with Mo, my wife, something catches my eye, and I stop to take a closer look. In a similar way, if in our reading of the Scriptures, something catches our attention, we do well to stop. This is the moment to dig a little around what we have noticed. Think of a miner who has spotted a little glimpse of gold. He stops, digs around the nugget and eases it out.

Don't be in a hurry to get a lot of reading done. We are coming to this book primarily to listen for the voice of God. So, if we see words or phrases in the text that are vying for our attention, it may be the first whisper of something God wants to say to us, or something He wants to teach us. At this point, stop and excavate.

We do not have to become fluent in the original languages of the Bible. There are some good books out there that can help us. Word study books help you understand the meaning of the original languages. Then there are dictionaries to explain things, concordances to suggest similar verses, and commentaries that show you the 'diggings' of others.

---

[6] Ralph Shallis, *From Now On*, (STL Books, Bromley, 1978), p. 100

Here is an example. At the end of John's Gospel, we read of a private conversation that Jesus had with Peter after breakfast. John wrote:

> When they had finished breakfast, Jesus said to Simon Peter, 'Simon, son of John, do you **love** me more than these?' He said to him, 'Yes, Lord; you know that I **love** you.' He said to him, 'Feed my lambs.' He said to him a second time, 'Simon, son of John, do you **love** me?' He said to him, 'Yes, Lord; you know that I **love** you.' He said to him, 'Tend my sheep.' He said to him the third time, 'Simon, son of John, do you **love** me?' Peter was grieved because he said to him the third time, 'Do you **love** me?' and he said to him, 'Lord, you know everything; you know that I **love** you.' Jesus said to him, 'Feed my sheep' (John 21:15–17; emphases mine).

In all our English versions you will find the word 'love' repeated. Here, I have highlighted them. The Greek texts reveal, however, that two different words for 'love' are used in the passage. They are firstly, *agapaō*, which describes 'a divinely inspired love that is sacrificial in nature.' The second word is *phileō*, which describes a 'deep friendship.'

Now set this into the context. In the courtyard of the high priest, Peter had denied three times knowing Jesus, and he was wounded by the fact he'd let his Master down. Now let me show you the passage again with the play on the two different Greek words for 'love':

> When they had finished breakfast, Jesus said to Simon Peter, 'Simon, son of John, do you ***agapaō*** me more than

these?' He said to him, 'Yes, Lord; you know that I *phileō* you.' He said to him, 'Feed my lambs.' He said to him a second time, 'Simon, son of John, do you *agapaō* me?' He said to him, 'Yes, Lord; you know that I *phileō* you.' He said to him, 'Tend my sheep.' He said to him the third time, 'Simon, son of John, do you *phileō* me?' Peter was grieved because he said to him the third time, 'Do you *phileō* me?' and he said to him, 'Lord, you know everything; you know that I *phileō* you.' Jesus said to him, 'Feed my sheep.'

So, what is happening here? On the first two occasions, Jesus is basically asking Peter, 'Do you love me enough to die for me?' Peter, still upset from his three denials, responds by saying, 'Lord, you're a good friend.' On the third occasion, Jesus meets Peter where he is at in his relationship with the Lord, and asks, 'Peter, am I your good friend?' Peter is broken again at this and responds, probably with tears, 'Lord, You know everything, I said that I would die for You, but I have realised that it is not in me. Right now, I see that I do not love You enough to die for You, but I am Your friend.' And, at that point of deep reality, Jesus recommissions him. A strong lesson here is that Jesus wants to work with us from where we really are rather than from where we think we ought to be.

There are thousands of nuggets like this lying just under the surface of the Scriptures. Charles Bridges in his book, *The Christian Ministry*, wrote, 'Study close; especially make the Bible your study. There is no knowledge which I am more desirous to increase in, than that. Men get wisdom by books, but wisdom towards God is to be gotten out of God's book, and that by digging. Most men do but walk on the surface of it, and pick up here and there a flower. Few dig into it. Read other books to help you understand that book.'[7]

Studying the Scriptures is taking the reading of them to a deeper level. Bridge's counsel to '...read other books to help you understand that book', is strategic. In my study, I have good books that I have collected over many years.

We must move from the glancing over the words of Scripture to actively engaging with them. If we are simply reading the words of the Bible, then those same words superficially enter our conscious minds and leave by the back door. They are then quickly forgotten. We must allow them to enter, and then we must learn to sit with them for a while and enjoy and also be challenged and changed by their presence.

Finger Three – Meditation

I hope you are getting the impression that we are slowing down in our engagement with the Bible. Now we move beyond reading and studying, to a place where we find time and space to start thinking more deeply about what we have been reading. In a nutshell, biblical meditation is about prayerfully pondering or musing over the words of Scripture. The Bible talks about Mary, the mother of Jesus, pondering over the things she had seen and heard (Luke 2:19).

Think of it as a pause in our reading. Perhaps certain words have caught our attention, and instead of rushing on to read more, we take a break and start giving serious thought to them,

---

[7] Cited by Charles Bridges, *The Christian Ministry*, (Banner of Truth, Edinburgh, 1976), p.51, note 1

asking God to open them up even more to us, allowing them to penetrate further into our hearts and mind.

The art of meditation in the Scriptures has a deep history in Hebrew spirituality. The book of Psalms opens with the words:

> Blessed is the man who walks not in the counsel of the wicked, nor stands in the way of sinners, nor sits in the seat of scoffers; but his delight is in the law of the LORD, and on his law he meditates day and night (Psalm 1:1,2).

I have written a devotional commentary on this psalm under the title 'The Song in the Gate.' In it I explain that the Hebrew word translated 'meditate' is *hâgâh*, (pronounced haw-gaw), which literally means, among other things, 'to growl'. It is the same 'growling with pleasure' sound that a dog makes when he is gnawing a bone. To meditate, we must gnaw on a scripture, spend time with it, allowing the text to enter us until we enter into it.

Alec Buchanan wrote, 'Meditation is the art of being still before God, and allowing the Spirit to speak to us through the Scriptures as we think over them slowly and carefully. It involves chewing and digesting the word until it gets from our head to our heart, thus affecting our will and conduct.'[8]

I will return to this aspect of reading in chapter nine.

---

[8] Alex Buchanan, *Bible meditation*, (Kingsway Publications, Eastbourne, 1987), p.16

Finger Four – Memorising

In our modern world, and especially in our western culture, much of this ability has been lost. Plato, the famous Greek philosopher, observed that when the spoken word was being taken over by the written word, the ability to memorise was going to be severely weakened.

I remember talking to a very experienced teacher in a primary school who made the comment, 'The moment that children learn to read, they start to forget.'

Bob Duerden also pointed out to me that the information technology industry, the internet and social media platforms have had a very similar effect. I think we need to recapture some lost ground.

Meditating on the Scriptures does help. Verses that have gone in deeply tend to remain within the memory, especially if we have rehearsed them aloud. Somehow, if the truths of God enter by what John Bunyan called 'the ear gate,'[9] they tend to linger. It is instructive to see how we can remember verses of songs that we have sung, and heard sung, but find it difficult to remember verses of the Bible.

Maybe that is why the apostle John spoke of reading aloud the words of Scripture. He wrote, 'Blessed is the one *who reads aloud* the words of this prophecy, and blessed are those who hear, and who keep what is written in it, for the time is near' (Revelation 1:3; emphasis mine). The Greek phrase is *ho anaginōskōn*, which refers to the public reading of Scriptures.

I earlier in this chapter that a Muslim boy is expected to have committed the whole of the Qur'an to memory by the time

---

[9] John Bunyan, *The Holy War*, (T. Nelson & Sons, Edinburgh, 1885), p.4,13

he has reached 14 years of age. Memorising the Scriptures can be done, and the earlier in life we start, the better. Start with some familiar verses and then build up to familiar passages. It is a forgotten discipline that needs to be rediscovered and practised.

If you find this hard, the learning centre in the University of North Carolina at Chapel Hill gives some valuable memorisation strategies.[10]

Finger Five – Practising Obedience

As I mentioned earlier, in the Hebrew language, the words 'hear' and 'obey' are the same word – *shâma*. From God's point of view, if there is no obedience, then His Word has not really been heard. Obedience is the spiritually natural outcome of hearing. Look at these Scriptures and notice the linking of hearing with doing (all emphases mine):

> 'Everyone then who *hears* these words of mine and *does* them will be like a wise man who built his house on the rock. And the rain fell, and the floods came, and the winds blew and beat on that house, but it did not fall, because it had been founded on the rock' (Matthew 7:24,25).

> ...a woman in the crowd raised her voice and said to him, 'Blessed is the womb that bore you, and the breasts at which you nursed!' But he said, 'Blessed rather are those who *hear* the word of God and *keep* it!' (Luke 11:27,28).

---

[10] https://learningcenter.unc.edu/tips-and-tools/enhancing-your-memory/

> But be *doers* of the word, and not *hearers* only, deceiving yourselves. For if anyone is a hearer of the word and not a doer, he is like a man who looks intently at his natural face in a mirror. For he looks at himself and goes away and at once forgets what he was like. But the one who looks into the perfect law, the law of liberty, and perseveres, being no hearer who forgets but a doer who acts, he will be blessed in his doing (James 1:22–25).

To get the best out of our Bible reading, we must put what we read and learn into practice. The most effective way of learning about love is by loving. The most effective way of learning about giving is by giving. And this is how it is with all the truths of the Bible. The practice of truth earths and ingrains the truth, and indeed verifies the truth.

The Bible is an amazing book. For the beginner, it can be hard work, but it is well worth the effort of persevering. Your faith will grow as you begin to understand who God is, and what He is up to. You will sense yourself being changed bit by bit. As you obey, you will understand more, and joy will come in the obedience. You will feel the strength of heaven in your heart and your mind.

Taking up the Bible with our hand, using the 'five fingers' mentioned above, we will find ourselves being drawn into a greater awareness of God and His workings. We will begin to sense the breath of heaven on our face. As we dig deeper, nuggets of truth will emerge. As we keep our spiritual eyes open, we will see things in the realms of the Spirit. As we keep our spiritual ears open, we may just hear His voice.

CHAPTER 8

THE VOICE OF GOD IN THE BIBLE

Honour the LORD, you heavenly beings; honour the LORD for His glory and strength. Honour the LORD for the glory of His name. Worship the LORD in the splendour of His holiness. The voice of the LORD echoes above the sea. The God of glory thunders. The LORD thunders over the mighty sea. The voice of the LORD is powerful; the voice of the LORD is majestic. The voice of the LORD splits the mighty cedars; the LORD shatters the cedars of Lebanon. He makes Lebanon's mountains skip like a calf; He makes Mount Hermon leap like a young wild ox. The voice of the LORD strikes with bolts of lightning. The voice of the LORD makes the barren wilderness quake; the LORD shakes the wilderness of Kadesh. The voice of the LORD twists mighty oaks and strips the forests bare. In His Temple everyone shouts, 'Glory!' (Psalm 29:1–9).

From within the pages of Holy Scripture, God's voice is to be heard by the attentive heart. It does not happen every time we open our Bibles, but Scripture is the primary vehicle through which His voice is heard.

It is not the only way He speaks. He speaks through creation. He speaks through prophets. He speaks through the preaching of the Word of God, and He speaks through conversations around a cup of coffee. He speaks through simple acts of kindness. The main thing to realise is that God is alive, and that He speaks.

If the primary way God speaks to us is through the Bible, and if we are to hear the Lord, then we must prioritise, and give time to, reading and meditating on the Scriptures. Frequent exposure to the Scriptures will put us in a place where the voice of the living God may be heard.

God wants to have appointments with us, usually in the mornings. He has things to say to us. I love Isaiah 50:4 in the Message Bible: 'He wakes me up in the morning, wakes me up, opens my ears to listen as one ready to take orders. The Master, GOD, opened my ears, and I didn't go back to sleep, didn't pull the covers back over my head.' On a personal note, whenever I come into my study in the morning, I open my Bible and say to God, 'Dear Lord, please find me sitting here before You, attentive to Your Word. Speak to my heart today.'

We engage with the Scriptures to deepen our awareness of God, to deepen our walk with Him, and to increase our understanding of His ways. We engage with the Scriptures to make ourselves available to God and to be open to His voice. If we don't engage, we won't hear.

We must learn to come to this book not just with our eyes open, but with our ears open. There are not only things to be seen in the realm of the Spirit, there are also things to be heard.

Reading with Our Ears

Back in the 1960s, I was one of two vocalists in a rock band. We were very loud and had earned ourselves the reputation of being one of the loudest bands on the South Coast. I also spent quite a few years as an apprentice in engineering workshops, which were full of noisy machinery. Many years later, I began to lose the top end of my hearing, and for some years now I have been wearing hearing aids. I sometimes say to those around me that I have the best of two worlds. When I put them in, I can hear the conversations around me. But when I am on my own, especially in my study, I take them out and I enjoy the quietness.

God is interested in our ears, because that is the foremost way that He speaks to us. Think about it: words are designed for ears, not eyes. Yes, there are things to see in the realms of the Spirit, but predominantly He speaks to us through words.

I believe we must recapture the art of listening. As we have already learned, the concept of obeying is linked with the hearing of the Word. If we are not putting what we have heard into obedient action, then it means that we have not truly heard. In this context, I am not speaking about audible hearing, but inaudible hearing. The Spirit of God speaks silently to our spirit. Very few hear an audible voice; mostly God's voice is unheard by the natural ear but is clearly heard by the spiritual ear.

There is a world of difference between noise in our physical ears and the voice of God in our inner ear. Yet the former can drown out the latter. One of the prerequisites for hearing the voice of God is having silence, not only around us, but deeply within us.

I have been helped by the works of some Roman Catholic writers, who demonstrate a Christlike life and deep love for the Scriptures.

One of them, Robert Cardinal Sarah, a prelate of the Roman Catholic church, wrote, 'Persons who live in noise are like dust swept along by the wind. They are slaves of a turmoil that destroys their relationship with God.'[1] There is a deep wisdom here that we do well to think on and absorb into our loud and frenetic worlds.

Augustine (AD 354–430) one of the earliest church theologians wrote, 'It is hard to find Christ in crowded places. We need solitude. If your heart is attentive, God allows himself to be seen. In the crowd you will find noise, in the silence you find God.'[2] David the psalmist wrote, 'For God alone my soul *waits in silence;* from Him comes my salvation. For God alone, my soul, *wait in silence*' (Psalm 62;1,5; emphases mine).

As I have walked with Jesus over these 50 plus years, I have learned to appreciate the place and environment of silence. It's not an age thing; it's because times of silence are when I hear His voice the clearest. I also find something else: Silence, to me, is not an empty space of God's absence. Rather, it can bring the intense manifesting of His presence.

---

[1] Robert Cardinal Sarah, *The Power of Silence*, (Ignatius Press, San Francisco, 2017), p.67
[2] https://www.clarepriory.org.uk/foa/thoughtsforlent.pdf

Like a lot of people, I have often found my ears becoming blocked with too much wax. When that happens, I find that I am not hearing too well, and the sound of the television keeps diminishing to the degree that I must keep turning it up a little more each day. However, when my ears have been treated, Mo, my wife, is exceedingly happy because the television can be turned back down to its proper level. There is a spiritual truth here. When my ears get filled up with the wrong stuff, I begin to lose my ability to hear the voice of God.

There is also the issue of internal noise. It is one thing to enter into a silent space, but quite another to still the voices, thoughts, feelings, distractions and emotions inside us. The cacophony of a busy life continues inside our minds long after voices cease.

I make no apologies for stressing this aspect of the spiritual life. Both solitude and silence are imperatives of the disciplined life that will take us to a greater apprehension of the presence and voice of God. These are disciplines that we need to learn to love and deeply appreciate.

The Three Switches

At this point, I am indebted to the work of Eugene Peterson. He made some very perceptive observations about three subtle, but spiritually dangerous switches which have taken place in modern society.

The Switch from Listening to Looking

We have become a consumerist society. This condition of the soul has also crept into the church. Instead of reading to listen and learn, we read in order to find something to use. We who preach on a regular basis can often skim through the pages of the Bible or even good books, looking for something that we can use for a sermon on a Sunday.

We find within church life a barely disguised undercurrent of our thinking that seeks to obtain something. We hear phrases such as: 'What can I get out of this meeting? What could I receive from this church? How will this worship service benefit me? What can I get out of this Bible?' Unfortunately, church leaders can pander to this, saying, 'What do the punters want?' In my view, that is the wrong question. A much better question is, 'What is God saying?'

Our attitude to the Bible, then, is of vital importance. We do not read the Scriptures to find something to use. We read them instead to have God speak to us personally, to challenge us, change our thinking and inform our belief. We must learn to come with a sense of awe, ready to hear His voice.

The Switch from Listening to Reading

Centuries ago, books were a rarity and only the rich could afford them; and so they were read with great care and attention. The advent of the printing press was a wonderful blessing in that millions of Bibles and books have been printed and distributed. But there is a downside to that. Now we are overwhelmed with books, and our minds have become inundated with what we have read. As we have noticed earlier, when we learn to read, we also find that we lose the ability to remember.

W.H. Auden (1907–1973) wrote these perceptive words:

This ease of access, when misused, becomes a curse. When we read more books, look at more pictures, listen to more music, than we can possibly absorb, the result of such gluttony is not a cultured mind, but a consuming one; what it reads, listens to, is immediately forgotten, leaving no more traces behind it than yesterday's newspaper.[3]

Today we live in an age of instant information. We are bombarded with texts, Facebook posts or memes and Instagram pictures. We can lose a lot of valuable time skimming through all the verbal and pictorial traffic. We can search Google and find out anything we want. The world is deafening us with information. We are in constant danger of mental and emotional overload.

On another note, when it comes to reading, we also need to notice who has the agenda. When I read, I have the agenda; when He speaks, He has the agenda. I can pick up a book, even the Bible, whenever I want to. But I cannot dictate when God speaks to me.

We must also beware when reading and studying the Bible, of treating it like a subject to be examined and dissected. Remember the analogy of the frog near the beginning of this book? If we cut something up, we run the risk of killing it. Though 'every detail of Scripture is worth pursuing endlessly'[4], if the Bible becomes a mere object of study, then we can miss the Lover speaking through the words.

---

[3] W.H. Auden, *Secondary Worlds,* (Random House, New York, 1968), p.128
[4] Eugene Peterson, *Eat this book,* (Hodder & Stoughton, London, 2006), p.46

The Switch from Apprentice to Student

They say that the best way to learn a trade is to be apprenticed to a master. Gone is the master/apprentice relationship where knowledge was passed on in an environment of relationship, watching and hearing the master's voice, as we worked alongside him or her. Now, information is given in large blocks to several people at once in a classroom setting. We currently sit in church auditoriums listening to sermons, or read books on our own, or listen to podcasts as we are driving to work. All these are good, in their rightful place, but maybe it is time to rediscover and rekindle the one-on-one relationship with the Master.

If we insist on doing all our learning in public settings or social and educational media platforms, we lose out on experiencing the personal, intimate relationship with the Lord that He desires.

Of course, our believing community is important. The Lord gave us the church to help authenticate, shape and deepen our walk with Him. But we must prioritise our personal walk of discipleship with Jesus Himself, hearing directly from His Word.

To sum up this section on the switches we need to make in our lives, hearing necessitates a relationship. We must learn to read with our ears so that our relationship with the Lord may be deepened. We read to hear the Master's voice.

The Faculty of the Spirit

In this section, I draw from the work of Watchman Nee, who constantly stressed the need to learn how to hear the voice of God in our spirit. In his insightful book, *Release of the Spirit*, he wrote, 'The Bible is more than words, ideas and thoughts. Thus the most outstanding feature of the Bible is that God's Spirit is released through this Book.'[5] The bottom line is this: God's Spirit inspired the Scriptures, and He still desires to speak to us through them. The conversation is from the Holy Spirit to our spirit. Let me explain.

Just as God is a trinity of the Father, Son and Holy Spirit, we are also tripartite in nature. We are body, soul and spirit. Paul wrote to the Thessalonians, 'Now may the God of peace himself sanctify you completely, and may your whole *spirit and soul and body* be kept blameless at the coming of our Lord Jesus Christ' (1 Thessalonians 5:23; emphasis mine). Notice the differentiating between the three elements of a person – spirit, soul and body.

Watchman Nee wrote, 'The spirit is the noblest part of man and occupies the innermost area of his being. The body is the lowest and takes the outermost place. Between these two dwells the soul, serving as their medium. The body is the outer shelter of the soul, while the soul is the outer sheath of the spirit.'[6]

Let us first look at **the body**. This is the human frame in which we live. It operates with the five senses of sight, smell, touch, taste and hearing. In the Bible it is called 'the house of clay' or 'the tent' in which we live and move and have our being. Job wrote of humans as those 'who dwell in houses of clay, whose foundation is in the dust...' (Job 4:19). He wrote of himself saying, 'I too was pinched off from a piece of clay' (Job 33:6).

---
[5] Watchman Nee, *Release of the Spirit*, (New Wine Press, Chichester, 1965), p.69
[6] Watchman Nee, *The Spiritual Man*, (Christian Fellowship Publishers, Inc, New York, 1977), p.27

Paul the apostle wrote, 'For we know that if the tent that is our earthly home is destroyed, we have a building from God, a house not made with hands, eternal in the heavens' (2 Corinthians 5:1). He clearly saw that this body was like a temporary tent that would not last forever. He looked forward to the day when 'the Lord Jesus Christ...will transform our lowly body to be like his glorious body' (Philippians 3:20,21).

When the apostle Peter wrote in his last letter, he knew that he was living in a body that would soon be put off or laid aside like a garment. He wrote, 'I think it right, as long as I am in this body, to stir you up by way of reminder, since I know that the putting off of my body will be soon, as our Lord Jesus Christ made clear to me' (2 Peter 1:13,14). Interestingly, the word that the ESV translates for 'body' is an old Greek word, *skēnōmati*, which is literally 'a tabernacle or tent'. The idea is of it being a temporary dwelling. Our current body, then, is the temporary structure in which we live. When it stops working and dies, it is laid aside, and we move on to put on a new heavenly and tangible body. In simple terms, death is the separating of the soul from our temporary earthly body, and the resettling of it in our eternal resurrection body.

Now, let us look at **the soul**. This is that part of us that is intrinsically who we are. This is our self-consciousness. You and I are living souls, living within our temporary bodies.

Our souls are also a kind of trinity. We find that within ourselves we have a mind, emotions and a will. The mind thinks, the emotions feel, and the will chooses. We have desires, and we appreciate things. The soul 'is the seat of our personality. The elements which make us human belong to the soul. Intellect, thought, ideals, love, emotion, discernment, choice, decision etc., are but various experiences of the soul.'[7] Our soul is who we are.

There is, however, something quite different about our soul. It seems to be in disagreement with the temporal nature of the body it lives in. At least, that is what I and others of my age feel at times. My daughter Sarah once asked me this question: 'Dad, how are you coping with getting older?' I thought for a moment and then replied, 'Good question! I feel like a 26-year-old driving around in a 70-year-old Mercedes-Benz.'

I think there's a reason for this feeling. Before the Genesis Flood, men and women lived for hundreds of years. Then, in Genesis 6:3, God declared a maximum of 120 years. After the Flood this began to greatly diminish until, according to the Psalm of Moses, 'The years of our life are seventy, or even by reason of strength eighty...' (Psalm 90:10). I think that there is a little something from the original creation of humankind lingering in our souls that feels that it is going to live for nearly a thousand years. After all, we were designed to live forever, living off the tree of life (Genesis 3:22). Because of the curse, that all changed, but there is still a distant echo.

Thirdly, let us look at our human **spirit**. This is that inner faculty that is touched by, and touches, God. I want to make much of this because this is the area of our lives where we hear the voice of God. Watchman Nee wrote, 'It is imperative that a believer knows he has a spirit, since...every communication of God occurs there. If a believer does not

---

[7] Watchman Nee, *The Spiritual Man*, (Christian Fellowship Publishers, Inc, New York, 1977), p.35

discern his own spirit he invariably is ignorant of how to commune with God in the spirit. He easily substitutes the thoughts and emotions of the soul for the works of the spirit.'[8]

True worship, therefore, is in the realm of our spirits. Jesus said to the woman at the well, '...the hour is coming, and is now here, when the true worshipers will worship the Father in spirit and truth, for the Father is seeking such people to worship him. God is spirit, and those who worship him must worship in spirit and truth' (John 4:23,24). Often, however, we mix our worship with soulish thoughts, feelings and desires. We need desperately to discern between the two dimensions.

Truth is communicated to us in the realms of our spirit. Paul, writing to the church in Rome, put it this way: 'The Spirit himself bears witness with our spirit that we are children of God' (Romans 8:16). Paul also served God in the realms of his spirit. In the same letter he wrote, 'For God is my witness, whom I serve with my spirit in the gospel of his Son...' (Romans 1:9). He operated in direct communication with God – the Holy Spirit speaking to his human spirit.

I understand it this way: We can safely say three things: firstly, the soul, **through the body**, is conscious of the physical world; secondly, the soul, **through itself**, is conscious of itself; thirdly, the soul, **through the spirit**, is conscious of God.

Before our conversion to Christ, we were only operating with two faculties – the body and the soul. Everything that shaped us came from outside of us, from what was going on around us. That would include our upbringing, the atmosphere

---

[8] Watchman Nee, *The Spiritual Man*, (Christian Fellowship Publishers, Inc, New York, 1977), p.31

around us, the words that we heard, the things that happened to us, etc., etc.. Yet within us, there was a void. Something was missing; the spirit.

Recall our earlier discussion of Adam and Eve in chapter three. When Adam and Eve sinned in the garden, something died within them both. They didn't immediately experience a bodily death – that would come much later – but something within them ceased to function.

Watchman Nee clarifies this when he describes the 'death' of the spirit as its incapacitation. It doesn't cease to exist, but it loses its sensitivity to God. 'Adam's spirit died because of his disobedience to God. He still had his spirit, yet it was dead to God for it had lost its spiritual instinct.'[9]

The Scripture says that God 'has put eternity into man's heart...' (Ecclesiastics 3:11). It is like an unresolvable ache. Augustine echoed this thought: '...for thou hast made us for thyself and restless is our heart until it comes to rest in thee.'[10] The void within is real. It is the dead faculty of our spirit. However, when we are born again by the working of the Spirit of God, this faculty of our spirit comes alive. That's what being 'born again' means. We find that now, from within us, there is a new voice, a new impulse, a new direction. God is beginning to impart the goodness of heaven into us. He is envisioning us, and He is empowering us. We are being spoken to and shaped from within.

---

[9] Watchman Nee, *The Spiritual Man*, (Christian Fellowship Publishers, Inc, New York, 1977), p.50
[10] Augustine of Hippo, *The Confessions of St Augustine*, (Andrew Melrose, London, 1905), p.1

The voice, and the awareness of God, comes to the spirit rather than to the mind. The mind then has to grasp it and frame it with words. The Holy Spirit communicates to our spirit. To illustrate this, we can turn to the writings of Paul the apostle. As we saw in chapter five, he wrote to the believers in Corinth about a profound spiritual experience he had in the Arabian desert. He spoke of hearing 'things that cannot be told, which man may not utter' (2 Corinthians 12:4). The NASB says that he 'heard inexpressible words.' The phrase Paul used was, *arrēta rēmata*, and it literally means 'unspeakable spoken words.' I think of these as imprints or impressions of the Spirit upon his spirit and, in this particular situation, they were too sacred to be uttered. They were communications of the Holy Spirit to his human spirit.

Paul also wrote to the Ephesians:

> For this reason, because I have heard of your faith in the Lord Jesus and your love toward all the saints, I do not cease to give thanks for you, remembering you in my prayers, that the God of our Lord Jesus Christ, the Father of glory, may give you a spirit of wisdom and of revelation in the knowledge of him, having the eyes of your hearts enlightened, that you may know what is the hope to which he has called you, what are the riches of his glorious inheritance in the saints, and what is the immeasurable greatness of his power toward us who believe... (Ephesians 1:15–18)

In a previous book, *The Church I See*, I discuss this verse as follows. 'The expression, "the eyes of the heart," is a beautiful metaphor, and is the stuff of poets. It is found only here in the whole of the New Testament.'[11] Two different dimensions are brought together into one phrase – the eyes and the heart. I recall Jesus' words in the sixth Beatitude: 'Blessed are the pure in heart, for they shall see God' (Matthew 5:8). Jesus links purity of heart with the vision of God. David does the same in the Psalms: 'The precepts of the LORD are right, rejoicing the heart; the commandment of the LORD is pure, enlightening the eyes' (Psalm 19:8).

Let me dig more deeply into this word 'enlightened'. Bear with me – it is important. The Greek word that Paul uses is *pephōtismenous*, and it contains the verb *phōtizō*, which means 'to give light, to illuminate.' That word comes from the root word *phōs*, which means 'light'. Some scholars say that *phos* and another Greek word, *phonē*, share the common root *phaō*, which means 'to shine.' The word *phonē* meant 'a voice.'[12] So there is a connection between light and voice.

Paul's conversion experience as he approached the city of Damascus illustrates this. Luke recorded, 'Now as he went on his way, he approached Damascus, and suddenly a light from heaven flashed around him. And falling to the ground he heard a voice saying to him, "Saul, Saul, why are you persecuting me?"' (Acts 9:3,4).

There was firstly a blinding light from heaven, and then he heard the voice of Jesus. Lying on the ground, he sought to grapple with the meaning of this powerful visitation. If we can extend Paul's experience to a mode of heaven's working, then it could be that (in the matter of revelation) there comes first a

---
[11] Alan Hoare, *The Church I See*, (Onwards and Upwards, Exeter, 2021), p.142
[12] *New American Exhaustive Concordance of the Bible*, (Holman Bible Publishers, Nashville, 1981), p.1692

flash of divine light upon our spirit, and then a voice – the voice of God. Something is seen and then something is heard. With Paul, the light shone around him, but I believe it illumined his spirit as well as his surroundings.

This, then, is how I feel it works. There comes a flash of light across our spirit, followed by a distinct inner voice. We see something and then we hear something. The revelation and the voice might seem to flit across our spirit, perhaps hovering there for a few seconds, but then it goes. To hear well, we must learn to listen well and try to capture the voice in prayer before it flees. Watchman Nee put it like this:

> God sheds light in your spirit, causing a burden in the spirit. The light flashes as a fleeting ray; it requires your thought to fix this light firmly or else it will simply fade away. After the thought succeeds in fixing the light, you need to seek God for words – perhaps just a few words – which can interpret that light. While thinking, you may think of some words which you can later write down. Or you sense something which you utter afterwards.[13]

At this point, I am grateful for the teaching of the late John Wimber and his team. Back in the 1980s I attended a three-day conference in Harrogate that they were holding. It proved a very significant time for me. Wimber taught that, in the matter of revelation by the Spirit, there are three stages:

The first is the **revelation** itself – what you see and hear – and it is usually very correct. This is followed by the second

---

[13] Watchman Nee, *The Ministry of God's Word*, (Christian Fellowship Publishers Inc, New York, 1971), p.46

stage, which is the **interpreting** of what you have seen and heard. It is at this point that our fallible human reasoning, mindsets and paradigms begin to speak to us, exerting an influence on our understanding of the revelation. The third stage is that of **applying** what we have seen, heard and understood. Yet again, our human judgments and predispositions can influence the outcome, colouring and even misdirecting the application.

This is why it is so important that we, firstly, know the Scriptures, and secondly, make ourselves accountable to seasoned and trusted leaders who know us well. They can often sense what is from the Lord rather than from our own hearts. If I think that I have seen and heard something from the Scriptures by the Spirit, I have always sought to share it first with my wife, and then with others whose discernment I have come to trust, before releasing it. This is a safety feature of church life. I also check it out with well-respected Bible commentators. This, to me, is acting responsibly and, because I am a pastor, it also protects the flock of God.

Personal mindsets and paradigms act as filters, determining what comes through. They also act like tinted lenses, putting a certain colour on what we feel God has said. There are three kinds of filters. The first are filters of *attitude*. This is about how we value the church and how we value the people in and around the church. Truth can be interpreted well but then spoken critically or harshly. We are called to speak the truth in love (Ephesians 4:15), so we need to guard our hearts, because whatever is in them will be mixed with the words that we speak in the name of the Lord.

Secondly, there are filters of *perception*. This is about how we personally view things. Our upbringing will play a huge part in this. We need to be aware that our perception, our point of view, our way of seeing something, is limited. God alone can see the whole picture.

Then there are filters of *personal agendas*. We can speak politically, defensively, and even culturally. In the Ephesians passage we considered above, there is the phrase, 'having the eyes of your hearts enlightened, that you may know...' (Ephesians 1: 18). I want to examine this word 'know'. The Greek word is *eido*, which properly means 'to see'. This is an ophthalmic word. There are things we can learn from books and classrooms, and there are things we can learn by experience, but this word describes when we 'see' something. It is 'when the spiritual penny drops'. It is a 'spiritual epiphany' or a 'eureka' moment. A.T. Robertson describes it as being 'able to see all these great truths'.[14]

A huge question for many of us is, 'How can I be sure that I am truly hearing God's voice?'

There are at least four kinds of voices out there that want to speak to us. There are the voices of significant others around us who express their opinion and perceptions. They can be wise and reassuring, or they can be negative and somewhat demoralising. They can be gently nudging us forward, or they can be locked into their own past experiences.

Other voices come from the realms of our own imagination. We can dream the dreams of God, becoming filled with godly vision, or we can dream our own fantasies, deceiving ourselves.

---

[14] Robertson's Word Pictures, e-sword.net

Here, we need to be brutally honest with ourselves and humble enough to seek the counsel of others.

Then there is the voice of Satan, the enemy of God. He appeals to our lower nature, offers us 'painless' shortcuts, and seeks to take us off track. We do well to be aware of his strategies. Do not think for one moment that he is an unbeliever. He was an observer at Creation, and he was outwitted and outraged by his defeat at the Cross and the subsequent Resurrection of Jesus. He knows who Jesus really is. He also knows the Scriptures better than any of us. A.W. Tozer wrote, 'The devil is a better theologian than all of us, and he is still a devil.'[15] He both accuses and confuses God's people. His words are destructive.

Finally, there is the true, clear, pure, and authentic voice of God. His voice leaves no confusion. His voice does not accuse or confuse us, but rather constructs, convicts and confirms us. His voice is full of kindness yet deeply penetrating. The more we live in the world of the Scriptures, the more we will learn to hear and recognise His voice. It will become familiar to us as we get to know Him through His living Word.

In the next chapter, I want to take us into an arena where God's Word can really penetrate the depths of our being, becoming part of us. Here, we will learn how to 'eat the word of God.'

---

[15] A.W. Tozer, *Man the Dwelling Place of God,* (CreateSpace Independent Publishing Platform, 2017), p.40

CHAPTER 9

GETTING IT INSIDE ME

In this chapter, I want to venture back nearly 1600 years to pre-medieval Christianity, seeking to bring to our attention a method of prayerfully reading and meditating in the Scriptures that is both ancient and effective in getting the Scriptures inside us. This is where we learn to absorb the Word of God deeply into our hearts and minds so that it becomes part of us, naturally working itself out in the way we think, feel and act. The more technical word is 'incarnating' the Word within us, allowing it to become enfleshed.

The method is called *lectio divina* (pronounced lex-ee-oh di-vee-nah), and the phrase is Latin in origin, meaning 'sacred reading.' The beginnings of *lectio divina* can be traced back to Origen around AD 220. He taught that to effectively read the Bible, one had to be giving the Scriptures our full and prayerful attention on a constant and regular basis.

The first organised system of *lectio divina* came about in the 12th century through the writings of Guigo II. He wrote a work entitled *Scala Claustralium* ('the Monk's Ladder'). In it, he outlined four steps that would take a monk from the things of earth to the sights of heaven. They were *lectio* (reading), *meditatio* (meditation), *oratio* (prayer) and *contemplatio* (contemplation).

This, however, was not designed to be a rigid system where one thing led to another, and all were experienced in one sitting! The Trappist monk, Thomas Keating, saw the four aspects as 'four moments along the circumference of a circle.'[1] The pattern is there, but it is flexible.

Going further than the 'gnawing on a bone' that I mentioned in chapter seven, this method of prayerfully and deeply reading the Scriptures can be likened to eating the words of God. In Hebrew, what we think of as the heart, they thought of as the stomach. In English we might say 'take something to heart,' meaning experience something deeply. They would say something similar to 'take something to stomach'. So, eating the words of God is allowing them to enter our hearts (stomachs!) and begin their holy influence with us. Jeremiah the prophet wrote, 'Your words were found and I ate them, and your words became to me a joy and the delight of my heart' (Jeremiah 15:16).

Ezekiel the prophet was told by God to eat a scroll that God gave him (Ezekiel 2:8–3:1–3). The apostle John was told to eat the scroll that was in the hand of the angel (Revelation 10:9). The words became part of them, influencing their hearts, their thinking, their prayers, their worship, their feelings, and shaping their ministries.

---

[1] Thomas Keating, retrieved from http://www.centeringprayer.com/lectio_divina.html

Let me remind us of some of our earlier thoughts about the preparation of our hearts. I do maintain that true spirituality is nurtured in the secret place or the hidden places. It is found and nourished in the quietness of a secret walk and conversation with God, but then it is authenticated in community. In this all the spiritual masters are agreed.

In our preparation for *lectio divina*, then, there are four important elements: Firstly, we need to find a time and a place. Then we need to create an atmosphere of faith *in* the Scriptures, respect *for* the Scriptures and an expectant attentiveness *to* the Scriptures.

A good opening prayer is the one of David: 'Open my eyes that I may behold wondrous things out of your law' (Psalm 119:18). We could put it this way: 'Open my mind to understand the Scriptures, to see them as You see them, and open my ears that I might hear Your voice.' (Read again these texts – Luke 24:45; Psalm 40:6, 50:4).

Here is another prayer that I sometimes use:

> Dear Lord, please open my eyes so that I may see wonderful things in Your word, vistas of the kingdom that will draw my heart after You, truths that will set me free and cause my heart to run after You.
>
> Please open my ears so that I may hear Your voice in the Scriptures, speaking affirming, challenging and even disturbing words that will both build me up and never let me settle into complacency.
>
> Please open my mind to understand the Scriptures, so that I may read them as You read them and see them

in the light of heaven. Please open my heart that I might receive Your words so that my life may be more conformed to Your image, that I might walk more fully in Your purposes and plans for me, and that I might partake and share even more in Your divine nature. Amen.

The purpose of *lectio divina* is to deepen our relationship with the Lord. The word 'devotional' points towards being relational, and we must constantly remember our primary calling is to walk in close relationship with Christ. The words of the Bible must enter deeply into our hearts and minds, drawing us, not simply into a deepened knowledge of Him, but into a deepened relationship with Him. We have already stated that we do not read Scripture primarily for biblical data or information, but in order to hear the voice of the living God. It is His voice that should be the springboard of everything we say or do.

In October 2007, I attended a spiritual retreat at Ampleforth Benedictine Abbey which was led by Father Christopher Gorst OSB (Order of St Benedict) on *lectio divina*. He taught that through the hearing and the absorbing of the Word of God, one was affected and transformed by that same Word until the incarnating of it had fully taken place. The truths of Scripture, in his view, were designed to shape us as well as inform us. They were to be assimilated in such a way that they became part of us. Through them, something of the divinity of God was to be communicated and imparted.

Peter the apostle wrote, 'he has granted to us his precious and very great promises, so that through them you may become *partakers of the divine nature...*' (2 Peter 1:4; emphasis mine). The *NLT* puts it this way: 'These are the promises that enable you to *share His divine nature*' (emphasis mine). Peter has carefully chosen the term 'nature' because it indicates growth, development and character. We don't, therefore, become like God in His essence; we do, however, become like Him in His nature. God has seeded us with His life and, by careful and prayerful exposure to His living word, we will grow to take on His likeness.

I remember sitting in the church at Ampleforth Abbey listening to the Benedictine brothers sing the psalms. In their manual, the 'Rule of St Benedict', Benedict instructed the brothers that, in whatever order they read them, 'one principle is preserved, namely that the whole psalter of one hundred and fifty psalms should be recited each week...'[2] As I sat among them, I was filled with the presence of the Word of God among them. Benedictines have continued this practice for about 1,500 years and, as a result, the atmosphere in the church seemed soaked in the Scriptures.

Stephen Binz, a Catholic biblical scholar wrote a wonderful book called *Conversing with God in Scripture*. I have found his writings very helpful indeed. Take time to ponder over some of the things he wrote. *Lectio divina...*

> ... lets us understand that our desire for God is the result of God's initiative, the stirring of God's grace within us, drawing us and inviting us to a deeper intimacy with him.

---

[2] Benedict of Nursia, *Saint Benedict's Rule*, (Ampleforth Abbey Press, Ampleforth, 1997), p.102

... continues the conversation that God has begun.

... allows the word of God to penetrate our hearts and leads us to grow in an intimate relationship with him. [3]

He also spoke of the way this practice helps us to love and linger over the text, until we are a 'biblical person... saturated with the words, images and memories of Scripture.' [4]

When we come to the Scriptures, our attitude and mindset is everything. We must approach with all those things we have already discussed: faith, teachability, obedience.

Let us now spend some time looking in depth at these four dimensions of *lectio divina*.

Lectio

The first movement is *lectio* – **reading**. The emphasis here is not on the amount of our reading but the depth of our reading. This will necessarily be slow. David Foster, in his book, *Reading with God – Lectio Divina* wrote, 'Speed reading is the absolute enemy of lectio divina.' [5] Lectio is the slow and deep reading of Scripture.

Here, then, we learn to read a passage slowly, lingering over the words. This will involve dealing with any impatience of spirit. It is a bit like letting a lozenge melt slowly in the mouth.

When we slow down, we find that we will see more. And so, when a word or a phrase catches our attention, we do not

---

[3] Stephen J. Binz, *Conversing with God in Scripture*, (The Word Among Us Press, Maryland, 2008), pp. 11, 13, 14
[4] Ibid, p.22
[5] David Foster, *Reading with God – Lectio Divina*, (Continuum, London, 2005), p.16

move on but stay with it. Sometimes it seems as if it is 'shimmering' – seeking to catch our eye. When that happens, we need to let it begin to touch our spirit, digging a little to get a better understanding. We need to learn how to 'wait on the Word.'

Michael Casey taught that repetition is the heart and soul of the practice of *lectio divina*. Words and phrases need to be read repeatedly. One look is never enough. Furthermore, we must slow down our reading to fully absorb the text. When this is done, we may catch sight of something we've never seen before.[6]

At this point I would like to share something that the Lord showed me several years ago. I call it *The vision of the yard brush and the shovel*:

> One day, whilst in my study, I saw myself standing with my back to the foot of a mountain. The Lord appeared beside me, and asked me, 'What do you see?' I replied, 'I see miles and miles of sandy desert.' He then gave me a yard brush and a shovel and told me to start sweeping six inches off the surface of the sand. I did this for a whole year, and when I returned to the mountain, I gazed at what I had done. To my surprise, I could see the outlines of roof tops and walls. I could see shadows beneath the sand. I said to myself, 'There is a city buried underneath the sand!'
>
> The Lord told me to repeat the process, and so, year after year, I would sweep another six inches off the sand. The city became clearer and clearer to my view.

---

[6] Michael Casey OSCO, *Sacred Reading*, (Liguori/Triumph, Missouri, 1996)

At one time, the Lord said to me, 'Stop here. Put down the yard brush, and take up the shovel, and dig down about twelve feet.' I did so, and found myself in a room, and sat opposite me was the apostle Paul. We spoke for a long time, and he opened up his heart to me. Then it was time to go, and I continued sweeping.

As the years rolled by, I swept and dug, and became quite familiar with the city. I encountered many biblical characters, conversing long with them. They were wonderful hours that I spent in their company, hearing their stories and their insights into the ways of God. At the end of my life, I stood at the foot of the mountain, and the Lord appeared to me again.

Immediately I was taken into heaven, and then, just as suddenly, I was back with Him at the foot of the mountain. 'Watch this,' He said. He then blew long and hard at the now partly submerged city, and to my astonishment, every grain of sand was blown away! The city stood before me in its pristine beauty – I had never imagined that it was so large and so lovely. He then said to me, 'Now enjoy the rest of eternity exploring it to the limits.'

Lectio is like this – a long, slow, sweeping which gradually reveals truths. It is full of wonderful discoveries but is only a glimpse of what is to come.

Meditation

The second movement is *meditatio* – **meditation**. This is where we look intently at, and muse over, a word or a verse in an atmosphere of quietness and prayer. Here, we learn to roll it around in our mind, thinking deeply on it, asking the Holy Spirit to 'enlighten' us (Ephesians 1:17,18). We start to reflect and ponder on the text of the passage, thinking about how to apply it to our own life. We learn how to gravitate towards a phrase or word that seems to be of particular importance. This should not be confused with exegesis (a critical and thorough examination of a text or passage of Scripture); but this is a very personal reading of the Scripture, where we let the text examine us!

Meditation is when we stay our minds on the text, pondering its meaning, and thus creating a way for the Word to penetrate deeply into our hearts. It is the deliberate, purposeful disciplining of our minds to think the thoughts of God, 'allowing the Holy Spirit to take the written Word and apply it as the living Word to the inner being.'[7] It is where the scroll we've eaten gets digested, converting the Word 'into real and proper nourishment.'[8]

It is good to start conversing with the text, asking questions such as, 'Who is speaking?' 'What was being said and heard by the original writers and listeners?' 'What is this saying to me?' At this point, let me refer you to Ignatian meditation. This is a form of meditation developed in the 16th century by the founder of the Jesuits, Ignatius of Loyola. Ignatian meditation makes creative use of our imagination through visualisation. The practitioner is encouraged to imagine oneself within a biblical scenario – 'as if you are there'. Then the

---

[7] Campbell McAlpine, *The Practice of Biblical Meditation*, (Marshall, Morgan and Scott, London, 1981), p.75
[8] Charles Bridges, *Psalm 119 – an Exposition*, (Banner of Truth, Edinburgh, 1977), p.31

practitioner is encouraged to ask the following questions: 'What can I hear?', 'What can I see?', 'What can I smell?', 'What can I touch?' and 'What can I taste?' We can use our imagination to hold a conversation with a character in the story that we are meditating upon, thus allowing the story to directly speak to us in fresh ways, often addressing situations of stress in our daily life.

One thing we need to consider at this point is that God has placed the responsibility of how and what we think firmly into our hands. It is true that we are often assailed by many thoughts that want to depress us and take us off track, but the apostle Paul clearly taught that Christians were to take every thought captive. He wrote to the church in Corinth, 'We destroy arguments and every lofty opinion raised against the knowledge of God, and *take every thought captive* to obey Christ...' (2 Corinthians 10:5; emphasis mine). In the book of Psalms, an unknown writer prays, 'When my anxious thoughts multiply within me, Thy consolations delight my soul' (Psalm 94:19 – NASB). It could also be translated, 'When I am entangled with troubling thoughts, Your consolations soothe and settle my soul.' We need to learn, therefore, how to bring and submit our anxious thoughts to God, and allow the truths of His Word to send a different signal to our minds.

The apostle Paul wrote often of the direction and subject matter of our thought life. He wrote about mindsets and spiritual food for thought. In Philippians he concludes, 'Finally, brothers, whatever is true, whatever is honourable, whatever is just, whatever is pure, whatever is lovely, whatever is commendable, if there is any excellence, if there is anything worthy of praise, *think about these things*' (Philippians 4:8; emphasis mine).

There is an interesting phrase in Paul's letter to the Ephesians. He prayed that the believers might be 'renewed in the spirit of your mind' (Ephesians 4:23). The word 'renewed' is the Greek word *ananeousthai*, which means 'made new from above, to be renovated by inward reformation.' Words from heaven have a cleansing, motivating, empowering, envisioning and shaping effect in our lives. But we need to note where the renewing takes place – it is not just in our mind, but in 'the spirit of the mind.'

The Scottish theologian, John Eadie, wrote, 'The change is not in the mind psychologically, either in its essence or in its operation; and neither is it in the mind as if it were a superficial change of opinion on points of doctrine or practice: but it is in the *spirit* of the mind; *in that which gives the mind both its bent and its material of thought...* in the power which, when changed itself, radically alters the entire sphere and operation of the inner mechanism'[9] (emphasis mine). As we prayerfully and slowly read and begin to meditate, we allow the words of Scripture to give us food for thought and fuel for prayer.

Oratio

The third movement is *oratio* – **prayer**. This is where we learn to respond to the Scriptures in prayer. As we read and begin to meditate, we will find a desire to respond to God with what we are seeing and hearing.

---

[9] John Eadie, *A Commentary on the Greek Text of the Epistle of Paul to the Ephesians*, (Robert Carter and Brothers, New York, 1861), pp.351.352

The important thing here is that we allow God to speak first. This, to me, is simply being respectful. It is rather presumptuous to talk to God before listening to Him. I have always been struck by King Solomon's words, 'Guard your steps when you go to the house of God. To draw near to listen is better than to offer the sacrifice of fools, for they do not know that they are doing evil. Be not rash with your mouth, nor let your heart be hasty to utter a word before God, for God is in heaven and you are on earth. *Therefore let your words be few*' (Ecclesiastes 5:1,2; emphasis mine). We should be slow to speak and quick to listen.

In my opinion, one of the best books ever written on prayer is the one simply entitled *Prayer* by Hans Urs Von Balthasar. In it he writes, 'The better we learn to pray, the more we are convinced that our halting utterance to God is but an answer to God's speech to us... Prayer is communication, in which God's word has the initiative, and we, at first, are simply listeners. Consequently, what we have to do is, *first, listen to God's word and then, through that word, learn how to answer*'[10] (emphasis mine).

Prayer, then, is 'replying' to God when He speaks to us through His Word. So often, however, we feel we must start the conversation with God. We talk to Him to get His attention, or to enlist His help in backing and supporting what we want to do for Him. Let us get this straight. Our prayers do not shape God's agenda, rather, we find that our prayers change and shape

---

[10] Hans Urs Von Balthasar, *Prayer*, (Geoffrey Chapman, London, 1961), p.12

us to fit God's agenda. Eugene Peterson wrote, 'If we pray without listening, we pray out of context.'[11]

I learned to talk by listening. My parents did not place a book in my hands and say, 'Read it and learn to speak.' I listened and I mimicked. I also remember when I first went on the Operation Mobilisation missions team to France. When we arrived at our destination, our team leader said, 'Now we are in France, we will only speak French to each other.' That completely shut me up! I had never learned French at school, and for those first few months in France, I struggled with the language. I could not get my head around the grammar, and so I listened. Like a child, I began to copy what I heard, and then practised it until my French team members understood me. Six months later, one of the French leaders said to me, as I was trying out my French on him, '*Alan, tu parles français comme une vache espagnole.*' (Alan, you speak French like a Spanish cow!) However, I persevered, and over the two years that I was there, I picked up the language well enough to converse, with a pretty good French accent! I cannot write letters, but I can certainly talk.

Language is spoken into us. We learn language by being spoken to. Probably the best way to learn to pray is by taking the words of the Psalms upon our lips. The fourth-century bishop of Alexandria, Athanasius, got it right when he said, 'Most of Scripture speaks to us; the Psalms speak for us.'[12] The book of Psalms is in fact a university of prayer for us all.

---

[11] Eugene Peterson, *Answering God*, (Harper & Row, San Francisco, 1989), p.53
[12] Eugene Peterson, *Eat this book*, (Hodder & Stoughton, London, 2006), p.104

In both Testaments we find examples of prayers that reflect the words and promises of Scripture. God's words are what we call 'architectonic': they are originating, initiating and constructing words, producing something that is both beautiful to behold and pleasing to the Lord. God, through His received words, originates, shapes and constructs the life of Christ in us. It does us good to dwell on them and to make them our own.

Therefore, we should let our meditation in the Scriptures shape our words to God. We will then find ourselves in a rhythm – synchronising with heaven. In doing so, we will begin to create an environment for revelation to occur.

Contemplatio

The fourth movement is *contemplatio* – **contemplation**. This word, in my view, has been somewhat abused by both the Evangelical and Charismatic / Pentecostal world, possibly because it has been misunderstood. Contemplation is a spiritual encounter that has a rich spiritual tradition beyond the early church fathers.

King David wrote, 'One thing have I asked of the LORD, that will I seek after: that I may dwell in the house of the LORD all the days of my life, to gaze upon the beauty of the LORD and to inquire in his temple' (Psalm 27:4). The word 'gaze' is the Hebrew word *châzâh*, and, according to the two Hebrew scholars, Keil and Delitzsch, it describes, 'a clinging, lingering, chained gaze.'[13] The word 'inquire' is the Hebrew word *bâqar*, which refers to 'a contemplative meditation that loses itself in God.'[14]

---

[13] Keil and Delitszch, *Commentary on the Old Testament* – e-sword.net
[14] Ibid.

Let me bring a thought about lingering. In the Gospel of John, chapter 20, there is the account of the two disciples, Peter and John, who were racing to the tomb where the body of Jesus had been laid. They had heard from Mary Magdalene that the tomb was now empty. The two men, followed by Mary, got to the tomb, went inside, had a look, and then went back to their homes. Mary, however, lingered. As a result, she was given the joy of seeing two angels and then the Lord Himself. Peter and John saw an empty tomb; Mary saw the risen Lord. If only they had waited!

There has been a wealth of solid teaching on contemplative spirituality, and I want to reference some of it from various streams of thought and experience. To various monastic orders, the word contemplation has a range of meanings. One is, 'resting in God,' in wordless silence. Father Desmond Tillyer, a retired Anglican vicar, wrote, 'what we are being led into is an intimate knowledge of God which is deeper than thoughts and words, concepts and ideas, and therefore remains inexpressible, and yet totally penetrating and transforming the soul.'[15]

The unknown psalmist of Psalm 119 wrote, 'Your testimonies are wonderful; therefore my soul keeps them' (Psalm 119:129). The word translated 'wonderful' is the Hebrew word *pele*, and it means 'that which is wonderful and seemingly paradoxical, exalted above everyday life and the common understanding.' The word translated 'keeps' is the Hebrew word *nâtsar*, and means, 'an attentive contemplation that is prolonged

---

[15] Desmond Tillyer, *Union with God – The Teaching of St John of the Cross*, (Mowbray, London, 1984), p.18

until a clear penetrating understanding of the matter is attained.'[16] Try putting those two concepts together!

Contemplation is also about deep union with God. This is a union where the Spirit of God embraces the human spirit. It is a divine communication at the deepest level of our being. Such a moment brings almost a displacement of our mind where, in our spirit, we see and experience something that the mind may not comprehend immediately. But, as we continue to gaze, words will form within us and an understanding will be given.

Contemplation is also about gazing into the face of God. This can be quite startling because, at times, we will experience God gazing into our own life. This is meeting with God face-to-face as it were, and such an experience can be life-changing.

The fruit of contemplation is clarity of vision and mission. We will find that not only is God gazing back at us, but He is also looking beyond us to those on His list. A true contemplative finds himself becoming mission-focused. Such a deep encounter with God must bear fruit. True contemplation will, therefore, thrust us to the front line of mission.

Kenneth Leech, in his book *Soul Friend*, feels that contemplatives are the clear eyes of the church, and feels that they need the most special care. He wrote:

> At heart, the contemplative is one who sees clearly, sees with the eye of God, the clear light which shines in the emptiness of the human spirit. It is clear vision which enables the truly spiritual man to see beneath the surface of events, to see through the illusion and phoney claims of human systems, to see beyond the

---

[16] Keil and Delitszch, *Commentary on the Old Testament* – e-sword.net

immediate and transient to the reality... For contemplative vision is revolutionary vision, and it is the achievement of the vision which is the fruit of true spiritual direction.[17]

I believe that contemplation is a gift. We cannot work ourselves into it, but we can make ourselves available to it by positioning ourselves openly before God. When imparted, we become very unaware of our surroundings and most aware of heaven. Things are then seen and heard that make a deep impression and increase our understanding.

Another New Testament word for this is 'trance.' Please do not become nervous of this word. It is thoroughly scriptural. The word used was *ekstasis*. The phrase can be literally read, 'an ecstasy.' The word *ekstasis* describes 'a displacement of the mind, a throwing of the mind out of its normal state.' It is as if you are removed from yourself, standing there starting from God, listening to words or impressions from God.

Kenneth Wuest translates the incident that happened to Peter on the rooftop in this way: 'While they were preparing the meal, *he entered into a new experience*, that of an individual whose attention has been drawn to and concentrated upon one thing *to the degree that he might as well be outside of his body so far as his physical senses registering anything is concerned*' (Acts 10:10; emphases mine).[18]

In Peter's case, it was as if God was saying, 'I want you to see something of My heart, and in this matter, I will throw your

---

[17] Kenneth Leech, *Soul Friend – A Study of Spirituality*, (Sheldon Press, London, 1980), p.191
[18] Kenneth Wuest, *The New Testament – An Expanded Translation*, (Eerdmans, Michigan, 2004), p.297

mind aside momentarily because it will actually hinder you. It will get in the way.' The vision happened, and Peter was left 'inwardly perplexed'. The Greek word used for 'perplexed' was *diaporeō* which meant 'to be entirely at a loss.' It is important to note that what Peter saw and heard confronted, challenged, instructed, and changed his predispositions. When our way of thinking rules, we can find ourselves limiting the workings of heaven.

Peter then went on to 'ponder' the vision. The Greek word used was *enthumeomai*, which literally meant 'inspired'. It also means 'to earnestly and passionately bring to the mind, to revolve in the mind'. Note carefully that the vision implanted in the realms of his spirit is now brought to the mind, and not the other way round. The unfolding circumstances then began to explain the vision as Peter followed the clear direction of the Spirit. When he entered the house and heard Cornelius' explanation, he said, 'Truly I understand...' The Greek word he used there was *katalambanō*, which means 'to take hold of so as to make it my own.' He had caught hold of the spiritual revelation with his mind.

Over the years, I have experienced a few occasions when suddenly I have become 'disengaged' from my surroundings and have seen and heard things from heaven. One such moment came whilst I was praying about an issue; another whilst I was in conversation with some friends; and a third when I was reading the Scriptures. There have been others, and they have all had a profound and lasting effect on me. They are forever etched in my spirit, and each time I recall them, they rise with their original clarity.

To sum up the four aspects of *lectio divina*, I find this simple poem by Dom Marion, a French Benedictine monk, helpful:[19]

We read...	(lectio)
Under the eye of God...	(meditatio)
Until the heart is touched...	(oratio)
And leaps to flame...	(contemplatio)

In conclusion, this ancient spiritual practice has one goal, and that is gradual transformation into the likeness of Christ – the living Word. What He is becomes embedded in us. We take on His likeness, His attitudes, and His thinking. A lifetime of deeply reading, meditating upon, and absorbing the Scriptures will eventually bring about a maturity and spiritual effectiveness that will act as a reference point for those around who are wavering in their beliefs.

May your heart become inflamed by the Word of God!

---

[19] Cited by Thelma Hall, *Too Deep for Words - Rediscovering Lectio Divina*, (Paulist Press, New York, 1988), p.44

Chapter 10

Constructing Solid Beliefs from the Bible

Many years ago, I wrote to a young lady who was beginning a three-year degree in Theology. I found myself penning these words to her: 'Deepen the fire within you...' It seemed an unusual phrase, but I felt it summed up what I was wanting for her. I felt that college would give the fire that was burning within her a depth and a framework. So, in this chapter we are going to look at how we can 'deepen the fire' – how we can give depth, longevity and a firm framework to our passion for the Lord.

At a leadership conference several years ago, Bob Mumford was asked this question, 'What is the greatest need of the charismatic church today?' I shall never forget his answer. Without a blink or a pause for thought he replied, 'The greatest need for the charismatic church today is theologians. There is a theology for what we believe, and it needs skilful men and women to lift it out of the Scriptures.' He went on to lament that 'Charismatics are far more experiential than theological.' We must be men and women who are full of both the Word of God and the Spirit of God, bringing depth to the fire within us.

Here is an interesting observation by R.C. Sproul: 'Countless times I have heard Christians say, "Why do I need to study doctrine or theology when all I need is Jesus?" My immediate reply is, "Who is Jesus?" As soon as we begin to answer this question, we are involved in doctrine and theology. No Christian can avoid theology. Every Christian is a theologian.'[1]

The apostle Paul, in his great letter to the Ephesian believers, wrote that God wants believers to grow in maturity 'so that we may no longer be children, tossed here and there by waves, and carried about by every wind of doctrine' (Ephesians 4:14). Writing to the church in Rome, concerning differences of opinion about holy days, he wrote, 'One person esteems one day as better than another, while another esteems all days alike. Each one should be fully convinced in his own mind' (Romans 14:5). The phrase 'fully convinced' is a translation of a long Greek compound word, *plērophoreisthō*, which means 'absolutely persuaded, convinced and assured'. Obviously, there was room for freedom of conscience, but Paul was insisting that they think through issues and come to considered conclusions. He did not want to see people wavering at the next conversation on the issue.

Paul also wrote to Timothy, 'But as for you, continue in what you have learned and have firmly believed, knowing from whom you learned it' (2 Timothy 3:14). There are two important terms here. The first is 'learned' and the second is 'firmly

---

[1] R.C. Sproul, *Knowing Scripture*, (IVP, Illinois, 2009), p.25

believed.' These describe the process. The phrase 'firmly believed' is the one Greek word *epistōthēs* (only used here in the New Testament) and it basically means 'to be convinced or firmly persuaded.' What is learned must penetrate deeply to become a conviction. We have to veer away from the penchant to be always and only learning new things. Truths learned must be mused over, meditated upon and prayerfully implanted by the work of the Holy Spirit. The study of theology, therefore, is about establishing convictions that will both sustain us and anchor us in the midst of the waves of shallow and often erroneous teaching.

There are many areas in the Bible which give rise to strong opinions on theological issues. We need to do our homework on them, coming to settled convictions as to what we believe. That is what theology is all about.

The writer of the letter to the Hebrews wrote,

> About this we have much to say, and it is hard to explain, since you have become dull of hearing. For though by this time you ought to be teachers, you need someone to teach you again the basic principles of the oracles of God. You need milk, not solid food, for everyone who lives on milk is unskilled in the word of righteousness, since he is a child. But solid food is for the mature, for those who have their powers of discernment trained by constant practice to distinguish good from evil. Therefore let us leave the elementary doctrine of Christ and go on to maturity, not laying again a foundation of repentance from dead works and of faith toward God, and of instruction about washings, the laying on of hands, the resurrection of the dead,

and eternal judgment. And this we will do if God permits (Hebrews 5:11–6:3).

There is also the very helpful Scripture found in Paul's first letter to Timothy which reads, 'If you put these things before the brothers, you will be a good servant of Christ Jesus, being trained in the words of the faith and of the good doctrine that you have followed' (1 Timothy 4:6). The word 'trained' is from the Greek word *entrephomenos*, which means 'constantly nourishing, educating and forming the mind'. It also carries the sense of 'feeding the mind'.

This 'diet' is two-fold: it is firstly 'the words of the faith' and then secondly, 'the good doctrine'. The former speaks of the sayings of Jesus and apostolic teachings that have been handed down. It is an unusual phrase, and it is found only here. The latter speaks of the whole body of wholesome and life-giving truths that have been formulated, and put in order, to facilitate the learning of them. These things nourish us.

Over many years of ministry, I have observed, even within myself, that people tend to get excited with the latest book they have read, or the most recent sermon they have heard. For those who are serious about all this, we must develop the habit of reading both new and old books. To be constantly looking for the new is to both disregard and disrespect the accrued wisdom of the great theological minds of the ages.

Without the deep earthing of the Scriptures, we can become quite cavalier in our theology. We've already discussed how a thorough knowledge of the Bible grounds us, sending deep and healthy roots into our hearts and minds, acting as an accurate sounding board to all the new things that we see and hear.

One other thing. I have heard so many people complain that the Bible is a difficult book to understand, and, yes, some of it is. I certainly would not recommend that you start reading the Bible in Leviticus! But once you're familiar with the 'easier' books, these others fall into place and will eventually help you comprehend why certain phrases and words are used. For example, the phrase, 'the blood of the Lamb' is only fully understood with a knowledge of the sacrificial system found in the Old Testament.

We must remember that the New Testament was written out of the context of the Old Testament. To fully understand the New Testament writing, we must be conversant with the teaching and concepts of the Old Testament. Jesus did not simply start something new; He was the fulfilment of what was already written.

My good friend Bob Duerden shared with me this little anonymous poetic piece:

> The New is in the Old contained;
> > the Old is in the New explained.
> The New is in the Old enfolded;
> > the Old is in the New unfolded.
> The New is in the Old concealed;
> > the Old is in the New revealed.

Before we start, let me introduce a very interesting word – 'perspicuity'. It simply means clearly and easily understandable. It was the term coined in the 16th century by the Reformers, who believed that the teachings of Scripture could be easily understood by any reader. To put it another way, anyone who is in a relationship with Christ, and is open to be taught by the Holy Spirit, will quickly find the Bible opening up to them.

So, let us make a start by looking at some important words and definitions, namely doctrine and theology. We will then look at different kinds of theologies, finishing with the formulating of good and healthy theology.

Doctrine – The Things to be Believed

Let me unpack this word. It comes from the Latin word *doctrina*, which is rooted in the word *doceo*, which means 'to teach'. Our English word 'doctrine' means, according to the Bloomsbury English Dictionary, 'A rule or principle that forms the basis of a belief, theory or policy; a body of ideas, particularly in religion, taught to people as truthful or correct.'[2] Doctrine then, is a developed body of teaching that forms a basis of belief and behaviour. It is then taught to others. The Hebrew word is *leqach*, and it means 'learning, teaching, or insight.' It is found in the book of Deuteronomy, in the song of Moses, where he recites the words, 'May my *teaching* drop as the rain, my speech distill as the dew, like gentle rain upon the tender grass, and like showers upon the herb' (Deuteronomy 32:2; emphasis mine). It is also found in the book of Job, where Job is reported to have said, 'My doctrine is pure' (Job 11:4). The word is rooted in the Hebrew word *lâqach*, which means 'to take in the hand, to lay hold of, to grasp.' The point, therefore, is that doctrine is a body of teaching that needs to be grasped firmly. To put it

---

[2] Bloomsbury English Dictionary, *Doctrine*, (Bloomsbury Publishing Plc, London, 2004), p.545

another way, we must know well, and have a firm grasp on, what we believe.

Most Christians do believe the Scriptures. It is one thing, however, to say that we believe the Scriptures; it is altogether another thing to know what the Scriptures teach. I have met many Bible-believing Christians who hardly ever pick up their Bibles. I have also met people in leadership positions in the church who have never read the whole of the Bible. One leader did not know where to find the book of Daniel.

Doctrine provides the framework for what we believe. Stephen Rees, writing in the Banner of Truth magazine, highlighted four reasons why Christians should study doctrine.[3] I have summarised them as follows:

Christians should become aware of the great doctrines of the Bible...

- because we love God and want to find out all that we can about Him;
- because what we believe shapes our spiritual lives;
- because it helps us understand the world we live in;
- because it helps us express clearly to others what we believe.

There is another very important factor to think about here. All that we know about God has been revealed by God. No one has discovered Him. Unless God reveals Himself, we shall never truly know Him. An important Scripture is where Jesus said to the disciples, 'All things have been handed over to me by my Father, and no one knows the Son except the Father, and no

---

[3] https://banneroftruth.org/uk/resources/articles/2009/why-is-doctrine-important/

one knows the Father except the Son and anyone *to whom the Son chooses to reveal him*' (Matthew 11:27; emphasis mine).

For the Hebrews, their body of revealed teaching was called the *tôrâh* (pronounced to-raw), often translated 'Law' (216 times). To them, the Law was given by God, and therefore was different from any other codes of belief and conduct of the times. If God had not spoken, nothing would have been heard and recorded. Heaven initiated the giving of the Law.

The Greek word for teaching or doctrine is *didaskalia*, which means 'teaching or instruction'. We find this word in Matthew's Gospel where Jesus said, 'This people honours me with their lips, but their heart is far from me; in vain do they worship me, teaching as doctrines the commandments of men' (Matthew 15:8,9). Here, in this instance, the teaching originated from the minds of men who manipulated the revealed words of God to suit their own ends. (The word is also used in Ephesians 4:14 / Colossians 2:22 / 1 Timothy 1:10; 4:1,6; 6:1,3 / 2 Timothy 4:3 / Titus 1:9.)

Another word is *didachē*, which also means 'teaching or doctrine' (Matthew 7:28 / Acts 2:42 / Revelation 2:14,15,24). We get our word 'didactic' from here. It can mean both the act of teaching and the body of teaching received. This can be put into two categories: 1) Teaching from an individual or a group, for example, the teaching of Jesus or Paul, and the teaching of the Pharisees or the apostles; 2) Teaching on certain subjects, such as the doctrine of the inspiration and authority of Scripture, of God, of man, of Christ, of the Holy Spirit, of salvation, of the church, of the end times, etc..

Yet another Greek word is *katēcheō*, which is simply another word for teaching. It is the origin behind the word 'catechesis'. The word *katēcheō* is constructed from two other words: *kata* (down) and *ēchos* (sound), together meaning 'to sound down into the ears'. It gives the impression of teaching that needs to be deeply heard and understood. It is found often in various forms in the New Testament. In Paul's letter to the Galatians, we find these words: 'One who is catechised must share all good things with the one who catechises' (Galatians 6:6 – literal translation). 'Catechism' was used by the early church to ground new believers in the faith. In a book written together, J.I. Packer and Gary Parrett wrote,

> Historically, the church's ministry of grounding new believers in the rudiments of Christianity has been known as catechesis. It is a ministry that has waxed and waned through the centuries. It flourished between the second and fifth centuries in the ancient church. Those who became Christians often moved into the faith from radically different backgrounds and worldviews. The churches rightly took such conversions seriously and sought to ensure that these life-revolutions were processed carefully, prayerfully, and intentionally, with thorough understanding at each stage.[4]

Theology

This word is not actually found in the Bible, but then neither are the words Trinity, Godhead, Incarnation or Deity, and yet

---

[4] J.I. Packer and Gary A. Parrett, *Grounded in the Gospel*, (Baker Books, Michigan, 2010), p.22

they are all important aspects of the Christian faith. The word 'theology' is taken from the Greek word *theologia*, a compound of two words, *theo* and *logia,* meaning 'speaking about God, or gods', or 'discourses about God', or 'an account of God'. Philo, a Jewish philosopher around the time of Christ, called Moses a *theologos* – 'one who spoke of God or God's spokesman'.[5] The Orthodox Church calls John the apostle, 'John the theologian.'

Good theology not only instructs the mind; it puts holy fire in the heart. Thomas Aquinas wrote, 'Theology is taught by God, teaches of God, and leads to God.'[6] In other words, theology is designed to deepen the relationship with God. The goals of theology are a deepening of our knowledge of God, our love for God and the heartfelt worship of God.

Nearly 50 years ago, I read something by A.W. Tozer in his penetrating book *The Divine Conquest*. It entered and became lodged in my heart and has shaped my attitude and understanding of theology: 'If a man has only correct doctrine to offer me I am sure to slip out at the first intermission to seek the company of someone who has seen for himself how lovely is the face of him who is the Rose of Sharon and the Lily of the Valley. Such a man can help me, and no one else can.'[7] Good theology will always draw your heart and attention to the Lord.

Dr Erik Thoennes wrote of the four categories of importance into which theological issues can fall.[8] I have reversed his order.

---

[5] http://embracedbytruth.com/THEOLOGY/Theologia.htm
[6] Cited in Richard Muller, *Dictionary of Latin and Greek Theological Terms,* (Baker, Michigan,1985), p. 299.
[7] A.W. Tozer, *The Divine Conquest*, (Oliphants, London, 1964), p.14
[8] https://www.crossway.org/articles/essential-vs-peripheral-doctrine/

We start with **questions**. These are the unsettled issues in our thinking about God and His ways. We have snippets of ideas drawn from a variety of sources, some of them not so reliable. As we investigate further, we develop **opinions**. These are vague, debatable issues that are not worth dividing over. Depending on our character, they can be either loosely held or ferociously held. As we delve for ourselves into the pages of the Bible, and sit under good teaching, we develop **convictions** that begin to shape what we think, what we do, and how we act within the context of church life. We then find the **absolutes**. These are the non-negotiables, or the core beliefs of our faith. As we have progressed in theology, we have moved from temporary floating ideas to deeply held and valued eternal truths.

There are different kinds of theology, and it is best to imagine them as different lenses examining the same truths. They can be described thus:

Biblical Theology

This discipline deals with biblical data **in a historic sense**, exhibiting the growth, development, and progression of doctrines from Genesis to Revelation.

For example, biblical theologians will write about how the doctrine of salvation unfolded over the years. They will use language such as 'the teaching about the Holy Spirit in *Genesis*;' '*John's* understanding of the *Logos* (Word); 'Faith as seen in the *letter to the Hebrews*.'

Gregg Allison, in a blog on the *Zondervan Academic online Theology course*, wrote, 'Biblical Theology looks at Scripture broadly, and reminds us that God does not give us the Bible all at once. Instead, God progressively reveals himself and his ways to his people over the course of time.'[9]

For example, in the beginning, when people began to relate to God, the meeting place was an altar. Later, that developed into meeting God in the tabernacle that Moses constructed under God's guidance. Following the tabernacle comes the temples – the first one built by Solomon, under God's guidance, then the one constructed in the days of Ezra and Nehemiah. That was followed by Herod's. The death and Resurrection of Christ brought about another temple called the church. This was the corporate temple, and alongside it came the concept of the temple of the individual, who was indwelt by the Holy Spirit. This Biblical Theology teaches us about how God related with His people throughout time.

Systematic Theology

This discipline deals with biblical data in **an orderly sense**, collecting and understanding all the relevant Biblical passages on various topics, then summarising them into an organised framework, so it is clear what one believes on each topic.[10] Simply put, Systematic Theology will show what the whole Bible teaches about God, Christ, the Holy Spirit, the church, the Second Coming etc.

Dogmatic Theology

This discipline is not unlike Systematic Theology, but it is in response to something. Think of this discipline as a preparation of biblical material both to answer and argue against errors that from time to time emerge and re-emerge in the life of the

---

[9] https://zondervanacademic.com/blog/what-is-historical-theology
[10] See Wayne Grudem, *Systematic Theology*, (IVP, Leicester, 1994)

church. Dogmatic Theology takes biblical data on any given subject and examines it thoroughly so as to make a waterproof case.

Historical Theology

This discipline deals with the insights gained, and the mistakes made, by others previously in understanding Scripture. It explores the historical contexts in which doctrines were formed. It gathers the development of key theological issues, taking into account the prayerful thinking of scholars past and present.

Liberation/Issue Theology

This kind of theology is to do with the emancipation of various subcultures within society. It is deeply linked with issues of injustice and basic human rights. At its best, it displays a deep heart for justice, and at its worst, it can incite angry and often intransigent pressure groups. Various theologies of this type include black theology that deals with issues of injustice on the basis of skin colour, feminist theology that deals with the recognition of female participation and leadership, gender theology, ecology theology, covenant theology, and so the list goes on.

This type of theology trawls the Scriptures for 'proof texts' for a specific issue and can become distrustful of mainstream theology. It begins to manifest itself with phrases like 'we have a theology for...' The issue becomes the lens of interpretation.

Philosophical Theology

Philosophical Theology deals with the understanding of right and wrong 'thought-forms' that are common in our culture. It mingles how we think with what God has revealed and what is going on in the world. It seeks to use philosophical reasoning processes to advance or defend the truths of Scripture. Quite close to this discipline is apologetics.

Apologetics

The word 'apologetics' comes from a legal Greek word *apologia*. In a court case, the prosecutor would deliver the *kategoria* (the accusation or charge) and the defendant or his lawyer responded with the *apologia* (the defence). This particular discipline deals with matching the teachings of Scripture with the objections of unbelievers, and then defending the truths of Scripture. It is primarily evangelistic in nature and seeks to uphold Christian beliefs against criticism and distortion, authenticating and clarifying the credibility of the truths of Christianity.

One of the great apologetic books of the last century is *Who Moved the Stone?* by Frank Morison. He was a journalist and novelist who grew up in Stratford-upon-Avon, England. He set out to write a book to discredit the Resurrection of Jesus and finished it by being overwhelmed with the various evidences of the Resurrection.

Another apologetic book is called *Evidence that Demands a Verdict* by Josh McDowell and his son Sean McDowell.[11] It is a book that puts well-reasoned arguments with evidential tools into the hands of believers to help them answer the many questions that non-believers pose.

---

[11] See Josh and Sean McDowell, *Evidence that Demands a Verdict*, (Authentic Media, Brighton, 2018)

The Bedrock of Theology

Theology has a history. Its primary and original purpose has always been to teach the truths of Scripture and to guard the church from error. Men and women will always have their own viewpoint of God and His ways. But when their own particular interpretation of the Scriptures becomes the major focus, error manifests itself.

Good theologians, according to J.I. Packer, are like water engineers and sewage specialists. He wrote, 'Their role is to detect and eliminate intellectual pollution, and to ensure… that God's life-giving truth flows pure and unpoisoned into Christian hearts. Their calling obliges them to act as the church's water engineers, seeking by their preaching, teaching and biblical exposition to make the flow of truth strong and steady; but it is particularly as disposers of spiritual sewage that I want to portray them.'[12]

It would be good, at this point, both to mention, and to spend time thinking about, the creeds. The word 'creed' is taken from the Latin word *credo* which simply means 'I believe'. During the first three to four hundred years of the history of the church, creeds were formulated to state clearly what the church believed in the face of heresies. The major ones are listed here, and it would be quite sensible to familiarise ourselves with them. (In these creeds, the term 'catholic' describes the universal church, not the Roman Catholic church.)

---

[12] Cited by Leland Ryken, *J.I. Packer – An Evangelical Life*, (Crossway, Illinios, 2015), p.336.

The Apostles' Creed

The 'Apostles' Creed' is the earliest referenced creed. Whilst it's unlikely it was actually apostolic in authorship, it was very much so in its content. Its present form represents an elaboration of baptismal formulas. Luther said of this creed, 'Christian truth could not possibly be put into a shorter and clearer statement.'[13] It has been called 'The Creed of Creeds.'

> I believe in God, the Father almighty, creator of heaven and earth.
>
> I believe in Jesus Christ, his only Son, our Lord. He was conceived by the power of the Holy Spirit and born of the Virgin Mary. He suffered under Pontius Pilate, was crucified, died, and was buried. He descended to the dead. On the third day he rose again. He ascended into heaven, and is seated at the right hand of the Father. He will come again to judge the living and the dead.
>
> I believe in the Holy Spirit, the holy catholic Church, the communion of saints, the forgiveness of sins, the resurrection of the body, and the life everlasting.[14]

The Nicene creed

This was an extended version of the Apostle's creed, approved in a longer form by the Council of Nicea (AD 325) but revised to its current shorter, and less condemnatory form, by the Council of Chalcedon (AD 451). It affirmed the unity of God, clarified the

---

[13] https://www.christianstudylibrary.org/article/who-needs-creed
[14] Common Worship, *The Apostles' Creed* (Church House Publishing, London, 2000), p.35

relationship between the Son and the Father and upheld the divinity of the Son and the Holy Spirit.

> We believe in one God, the Father, the Almighty, maker of heaven and earth, of all that is, seen and unseen.
>
> We believe in one Lord, Jesus Christ, the only Son of God, eternally begotten of the Father, God from God, Light from Light, true God from true God, begotten, not made, of one being with the Father.
>
> Through him all things were made. For us and for our salvation he came down from heaven: by the power of the Holy Spirit he became incarnate from the Virgin Mary, and was made man.
>
> For our sake he was crucified under Pontius Pilate; he suffered death and was buried. On the third day he rose again in accordance with the Scriptures; he ascended into heaven and is seated at the right hand of the Father. He will come again in glory to judge the living and the dead, and his kingdom will have no end.
>
> We believe in the Holy Spirit, the Lord, the giver of life, who proceeds from the Father and the Son. With the Father and the Son he is worshiped and glorified. He has spoken through the Prophets. We believe in one holy catholic and apostolic Church. We acknowledge one baptism for the forgiveness of sins. We look for the resurrection of the dead, and the life of the world to come. Amen.[15]

---

[15] Common Worship, *The Nicene Creed*, (Church House Publishing, London, 2000), p.140

The Athanasian creed

Although named after Athanasius, the 4th century bishop of Alexandria, this creed was written by an unknown author of the Augustinian tradition in the 5th century. It contains a clear and concise statement of the Trinity and the Incarnation. It is very lengthy and somewhat wordy but can be found online or in the appendix to Wayne Grudem's *Systematic Theology*.[16]

These creeds, and others, were used for baptismal confessions, for teaching, for refutation of error, and for liturgy in services. They are part of the rich heritage from the serious and prayerful thought of early theologians.

The Formulating of Theology

Biblical truths are scattered throughout the Scriptures, and there is a need for orderly studies. A helpful analogy is that of a jigsaw puzzle. Scattered about are all the pieces that make up the picture. Formulating theology is like putting in the borders and the main features thus helping us to fill in the gaps more easily. So how do we start to put together a thorough, well-thought-through and biblical framework of belief?

At this point, I want to draw on the excellent work of three theologians: William Klein, Craig Blomberg and Robert Hubbard. I have adapted their thoughts on the subject.

We Formulate Theology from what God has Revealed

We must remember that the Scriptures are inspired by God and as such they contain the revelation of God. The Bible is a

---

[16] Wayne Grudem, *Systematic Theology*, (Zondervan, Michigan, 1994), pp.1170,1171

deeply spiritual book that can only be truly understood with the help of the Holy Spirit.

Natural thinking will take us so far, but it will never take us to the heart and core of God and His kingdom. Studies in other fields (archaeology, ancient history, linguistics) have shed helpful light, but they must not form the basis of our theological studies. Our theology must come from the Scriptures. Klein, Blomberg and Hubbard wrote, '...unless theology rests upon solid biblical foundations, it exists only as a monument to human brilliance.'[17] Furthermore, it must be formulated from the whole Bible, and not just from isolated or carefully selected texts. The whole Bible must be read, and God must be allowed to speak for Himself.

We Formulate Theology with Prayer

It's been said, 'It's not more data we need, it's insight into the data we already have.' There is a certain amount that we can deduce by ourselves, but to truly know God and His ways means that we must ask Him to reveal Himself to us by His Spirit, and to give us insight into the Scriptures. Concerning the wisdom that comes from God, Charles Bridges wrote, 'Earthly wisdom is gained by study, heavenly wisdom by prayer. Study may form a biblical scholar; prayer puts the heart under a heavenly tutelage.'[18] We need to ask the Holy Spirit to teach us and to open our hearts and our understanding to the truths of Scripture. We formulate theology prayerfully.

---

[17] Klein, Blomberg, Hubbard, *Introduction to Biblical Interpretation*, (Word Publishing, Dallas, 1993), p.389
[18] Charles Bridges, *Proverbs*, (Banner of Truth, Edinburgh, 1977), p.14

We Formulate Theology with Humility

David the psalmist wrote, 'He leads the humble in what is right, and teaches the humble his way' (Psalm 25:9). We must come to this book with a humble and teachable spirit. Dr R.A. Torrey wrote, 'Do not come to the Bible full of your own ideas and seeking from it a confirmation of them. Come rather to find out what are God's ideas as He has revealed them there. Come not to find a confirmation of your own opinion, but to be taught what God may be pleased to teach.'[19] This is of the utmost importance. We must not just seek to get a handle on the Bible. We must let the Bible get a handle on us!

Theologians talk about antimonies. These are biblical truths which, on the surface, seem irreconcilable. For example, the centuries-old debate about the free will of man and the sovereignty of God. Both doctrines are truths exegeted from the Bible. Many godly and able scholars have wrestled with these two truths and have concluded that they are fully reconciled only in heaven. But that does not prevent us from applying their truths to our lives.

We also must acknowledge the frailty and inadequacy of our human thinking. We will never arrive at a total understanding of God and His ways this side of heaven, therefore, for the whole of our lives here on earth we will be learners. The longer I spend reading the Scriptures, the more I realise how little I know. Ponder these words from the Scriptures: 'Great is the LORD, and greatly to be praised, and his greatness is unsearchable' (Psalm 145:3). 'Oh, the depth of the riches and wisdom and knowledge of God! How unsearchable

---

[19] R.A. Torrey, *How to study the Bible*, (Oliphants Ltd, London, 1955), p.105

are his judgments and how inscrutable his ways!' (Romans 11:33).

We must come to terms with the fact that there will always be gaps in our thinking. Indeed, there will be in any theological system. On this side of life, we cannot know everything. To say that we do not know all the answers to every question exhibits a genuine humility.

We Formulate Theology with the Help of Others

We must not work in isolation. Many others have worked on, and thought deeply about Scripture. Much can be lost by ignoring their contributions and their insights. Our theology must be worked out in both verbal and silent dialogue with the creeds of the church, the traditions passed down from apostolic days and in consultation with both current and historical theological thinking. If we ignore the insights and the wisdom from the past, our future thinking can be quickly derailed.

All revelation should be weighed by those who are older than us in the faith. Follow this process through with the apostle Paul in his letter to the Galatians. Firstly, he believed that his calling and the revelation of Christ and the church came directly from Christ Himself:

> Paul, an apostle—not from men nor through man, but through Jesus Christ and God the Father, who raised him from the dead... (Galatians 1:1).

> For I would have you know, brothers, that the gospel that was preached by me is not man's gospel. For I did not receive it from any man, nor was I taught it, but I

> received it through a revelation of Jesus Christ. (Galatians 1:11,12).
>
> But when he who had set me apart before I was born, and who called me by his grace, was pleased to reveal his Son to me, in order that I might preach him among the Gentiles, I did not immediately consult with anyone... (Galatians 1:15,16).

He then submitted his teaching to the apostolic leadership in Jerusalem:

> Then after fourteen years I went up again to Jerusalem with Barnabas, taking Titus along with me. I went up because of a revelation and set before them (though privately before those who seemed influential) the gospel that I proclaim among the Gentiles, in order to make sure I was not running or had not run in vain. (Galatians 2:1,2).

At the time of writing, I have been doing some personal study on the first seven verses of the book of Proverbs. I began by writing, 'The other morning, I got into my study and opened up my Bible to the book of Proverbs. I have read this book many times, and I was looking forward to musing my way through the layers of wisdom in it. Suddenly, in my spirit, I saw myself standing on the brink of the Grand Canyon in Arizona. It was vast, and I knew that it would takes weeks, maybe months to explore it completely. That was the feeling that I had as I looked upon the beginning of this book. I fought off the thoughts of not going for it because of the time that it would take, feeling that perhaps this time round, I could just skim the surface. But then I thought better of it and took the plunge as it were. *I decided to do it in company with some theologians.* I have on my shelf commentaries written by serious scholars on the book of Proverbs. One of them was written in 1846. I wanted to compare and check my own findings with theirs and, where necessary, be corrected by them.

We Formulate Theology with Reason

Revelation and reason are not enemies. In fact, they love to walk together. But there is an order. Reason does not inform revelation but rather it is the other way around. Reason needs to follow revelation. My favourite monk, Thomas à Kempis, in his book *The Imitation of Christ* focuses on the communion service in the last chapter, and he wrote of the submission of reason to faith: 'Whatever you cannot understand commit to the security of the all-powerful God, who does not deceive you. The man, whoever, who trusts in himself is deceived. God walks with sincere men, reveals himself to humble men, enlightens the understandings of pure minds, and hides his grace from the curious and the proud. Human reason is weak and can be deceived. *All reason and natural science ought to come after faith, not go before it, nor oppose* it'[20] (emphasis mine).

Jesus said that the greatest commandment was to love God 'with all your heart and with all your soul and *with all your mind*' (Matthew 22;37; emphasis mine). God expects us to think, and to love Him with our thinking. Thinking is part of who we are. Good theology is not done with our feelings or emotions.

---

[20] Thomas à Kempis, *The Imitation of Christ*, (Hendrickson Publishers, Massachusetts, 2004), p.160

To say 'it feels right' is bad theology. Our thinking must lead our emotions, and not the other way around.

In chapter 5 we spoke of how Jesus drew alongside two disconsolate disciples walking back to Emmaus after His Resurrection. He shared with them the Scriptures that spoke of Himself, and they testified later, 'Did not our hearts burn within us while he talked to us on the road, while he opened to us the Scriptures?' (Luke 24:32). Later, when He met with the disciples behind closed doors, it is written that He 'opened their minds to understand the Scriptures' (Luke 24:45). The Scriptures were opened to heal, inflame and inspire their hearts, but their minds were opened to understand the Scriptures. We need both: hearts on fire and understanding minds.

Opening the book

Now to the Bible itself. To formulate theology, we must **observe** what is written within its pages. This is done, firstly, by prayerfully reading the text and seeing how it is set within its context. It has been said that a text taken out of its context quickly becomes a pretext. We need to build a bridge by understanding the culture of the day and the historical background. This will help us comprehend what the original hearers would have understood from what they heard. Seek to get back into their world.

Secondly, as much as you can, **examine** the meanings of the words in their original languages. At the end of this book, I have added an appendix showing recommended books to help you do that. Sometimes, the English language will provide one word, whereas in the original language, two different ones are used. We looked at an example earlier when Jesus spoke to Peter. Here's another one:

> Everyone then who hears these words of mine and does them will be like a wise man who built his house on the rock. And the rain fell, and the floods came, and the winds blew and beat [*prospiptō*] on that house, but it did not fall, because it had been founded on the rock. And everyone who hears these words of mine and does not do them will be like a foolish man who built his house on the sand. And the rain fell, and the floods came, and the winds blew and beat [*proskoptō*] against that house, and it fell, and great was the fall of it (Matthew 7:24–27).

In the ESV translation, the two phrases 'beat on' and 'beat against' are used. They translate two totally different Greek words. For the one who 'hears and does', the phrase 'beat on' translates the Greek word *prospiptō*, which literally means, 'to trip, fall, to prostrate oneself before something or someone.' On the other hand, for the one who 'hears and does not do', the phrase 'beat against' translates the Greek word *proskoptō*, which means 'to strike against.' I particularly like the translation of this text in the J.B. Phillips version of the New Testament. In the case of the practising hearer, the winds 'blew and roared upon that house...' In the case of the non-practising hearer, the winds 'blew and battered that house until it collapsed...'[21]

My theological point is this: The very same storms that strike and flatten the house of the non-practising hearer will in

---

[21] J.B. Phillips, *The New Testament in Modern English*, (Godfrey Bles, London, 1960), p. 13

fact trip and fall before the house of the practising hearer. Disobedience will leave us vulnerable; obedience will protect us. In that light, have another think about what that parable would have meant to the original hearers.

Thirdly, **compare** your findings with what other theologians and scholars have written. Compare your notes with their observations. Do not rely purely on the latest studies but compare with the older and more seasoned thinkers.

Next, we get into the realm of **interpreting** what we have found, and to be honest, this is where our 'humanness' comes in. We all have different ways of looking at things, coming at the texts from different angles. Theologians talk about 'pre-understandings' and 'presuppositions.' We must never read our own pre-understandings into the Scriptures; rather, we must allow the Scriptures to alter and enlarge our own worldview. I knew a South African student who was shocked one Christmas to see snow falling from the sky. Her only previous encounter with snow had been with a photograph and she had assumed that snow came up like dew!

We need to know ourselves, and our own historical setting and culture, as we approach the text and the world of the text. Dr D.S. Ferguson outlined four basic categories of pre-understanding, and I have put his thinking in my own words.[22]

The first is **informational**. This is what we already think we know about the subject before we approach it. The second is **attitudinal**. This can be our own personal prejudice, bias, predisposition or state of mind. The third is **ideological**. This is

---

[22] D.S. Ferguson, *Biblical Hermeneutics: An Introduction*, (John Knox, Atlanta, 1986), p.12

our own worldview, our personal frame of reference, or even our point of view on any subject. It is a well-attested fact that no one ever sees the same rainbow – we all see it from a different angle. Different approaches can influence the outcomes that we seek. The final category is **methodological**. This is the actual approach we take to the subject, of which scientific, historical or inductive methodologies are numbered.

A good theology requires an open-hearted receptivity to the Scriptures. A good theologian is ever open to a transformative change of thinking to any presuppositions.

Applying the book

We may gain a lot of information from our studies, but it is only fully learned when we apply it to our own lives. Using the Scripture cited above from Matthew 7:24–27, Jesus said that the wise were those who both heard and put into practice the words that He spoke. James, the half-brother of Jesus, said something similar when he wrote:

> But be doers of the word, and not hearers only, deceiving yourselves. For if anyone is a hearer of the word and not a doer, he is like a man who looks intently at his natural face in a mirror. For he looks at himself and goes away and at once forgets what he was like. But the one who looks into the perfect law, the law of liberty, and perseveres, being no hearer who forgets but a doer who acts, he will be blessed in his doing (James 1:22–25).

Furthermore, we must never seek to apply what we have learned to others until we have firstly applied it to ourselves.

We must not become high thinking academic theorists but aim to be deeply rooted practitioners. All that we see and understand from the Scriptures must be translated into our daily living. When detached from life and divorced from practical implementation, theology becomes cold and sterile, and fails to bring into fruition the purposes of God which are to transform lives, not just inform them. When the apostle Paul wrote that, 'All Scripture is breathed out by God and profitable for teaching, for reproof, for correction, and for training in righteousness, that the man of God may be complete, equipped for every good work' (2 Timothy 3:16), he was stating the Scriptures had definite purpose. He also wrote to Titus of the 'knowledge of the truth, which accords with godliness...' (Titus 1:1). Here, he was saying that the knowledge of the truth must be congruent with, and produce, godly lives. Godly precepts must result in godly lifestyles.

And Finally...

So, why do we want to study and formulate theology? Here are five very good reasons:

1) Studying and formulating theology helps us understand and thereby worship the God we believe in. True theology will lead us to stand before God in awe and worship. True theology will cause a song to rise within our hearts. J.I. Packer wrote, 'The older I get, the more I want to sing my faith and get others singing with me... the first thing I want to do with [theology] is turn it into praise and thus honour the God who is its subject.'[23]

---

[23] J. I. Packer, *God has Spoken*, (Hodder & Stoughton, London, 1979), p.7

2) Studying and formulating theology helps us understand what the whole Bible teaches on many different subjects. There is a calling on us, not just to be familiar with one or two favourite passages, but to have an intimate working knowledge of all the Scriptures. Two of my personal heroes in the Bible are Ezra and Apollos. I mentioned Ezra earlier, and his skill in the Law of Moses. Because he knew the Scriptures so thoroughly, he was able to quickly refer to them in any given situation. Because he 'had set his heart to study the law of the Lord, and to practise it', Ezra did not have to fumble (Ezra 7:10). The Scriptures were deeply ingrained in him; they were at his fingertips.

Notice that Ezra *set his heart* to study the law. This speaks of a deliberate, chosen, determined direction of life. Doing theology properly for Ezra was not a five-minute wonder, a spur of the moment experience; it was applying himself diligently and purposefully for his lifetime. Secondly, his teaching carried weight, because he had practised in his own life what he had learned.

In a similar way it was written of Apollos that 'He was an eloquent man, competent in the Scriptures. He had been instructed in the way of the Lord. And being fervent in spirit, he spoke and taught accurately the things concerning Jesus, though he knew only the baptism of John' (Acts 18:24,25). The word translated 'eloquent' is the Greek word *logios*, which means 'learned, skilled in speech, fluent.' The English word 'competent' is translated from the Greek word *dunatos*, which means 'able, powerful, mighty, strong.' The KJV has it that he was 'mighty in the Scriptures.'

What I love about Apollos is that he remained teachable. Luke's account in Acts tells us that 'He began to speak boldly in the synagogue, but when Priscilla and Aquila heard him, they took him aside and explained to him the way of God more accurately' (Acts 18:26). Good teachers are always learning; great teachers are easily correctable. Apollos was a wise man. Solomon wrote, 'reprove a wise man, and he will love you. Give instruction to a wise man, and he will be still wiser; teach a righteous man, and he will increase in learning' (Proverbs 9:8,9).

3) Studying and formulating theology will help us overcome wrong thinking. In chapter seven, I quoted George Müller teaching that, 'a continuous reading of the Scriptures will reveal God's thoughts in their variety and connections, *and will go far to correct erroneous views*'[24] (emphasis mine). Keeping in mind a theological framework as we read can also protect us from drawing incorrect conclusions from what we read.

4) Studying and formulating theology helps us to be better prepared for the future. Instead of being blown off course by new winds of doctrine, we will be able to weigh them against the truths of the Bible. Our footings will be more solid. Paul had to do this with the believers in Thessalonica. In his day, some were teaching that the return of Christ had already happened, so he corrected their thinking (2 Thessalonians 2:15).

5) Studying and formulating theology will help us to grow in personal maturity. I am convinced that Charles Spurgeon was right when he said, 'A Bible that's falling apart usually belongs to someone who isn't.'[25] Somebody else put it this way: 'When a

---

[24] A.T. Pierson, *George Müller of Bristol*, (Pantianos Classics, first published 1899), pp.168,169
[25] https://www.goodreads.com/quotes/397346

man's Bible is falling apart, it's a pretty good sign that he is well put together!'

Building Your Tool Kit

I have met musicians who have spent thousands of pounds on musical instruments, amplifiers, and pedals. If I walk into my friend Neal's workshop (apart from leading a church, he is a Jaguar specialist and a restorer of vintage cars), I see thousands of pounds worth of tools and equipment. Over the years, I have built my own library. It is full of commentaries, dictionaries, and various other study books. If I had it valued, it would run into thousands of pounds worth of books. If you are going to take something seriously, you will wish to invest in it over the years.

If you are going to start seriously getting into your Bible and getting your Bible into you, then I suggest that you think about putting together a basic Bible toolkit (see the appendix for my specific suggestions):

- A Study Bible with notes, illustrations, and maps
- A Concordance (An alphabetical index of the words in the Bible and where they are found)
- Books on reading the Bible
- Whole Bible Commentaries
- Bible Dictionaries
- Systematic Theology books

All of these can be purchased from any good Christian bookstore or online. Many of them, to help your budget, can be bought second-hand in a pretty good condition.

Next there are the books on various subjects. Choose them wisely, doing a background check on the authors, looking to see who endorses their work. As I wrote earlier, do not limit your reading to the latest books that have just come on the market. C.S. Lewis wrote, 'It is a good rule, after reading a new book, never to allow yourself another new one till you have read an old one in between. If that is too much for you, you should at least read one old one to every three new ones. Every age has its own outlook. It is especially good at seeing certain truths and specially liable to make certain mistakes. We all, therefore, need the books that will correct the characteristic mistakes of our own period. And that means the old books.'[26]

A basic structure of theological subjects

Here is a framework on which to build. These are areas of study that, if looked at carefully and thoughtfully, will equip you with a good understanding of what the Bible teaches:

- The doctrine of Scripture. Its history, its authority and inspiration.
- The doctrine of God. His nature, character, and personality.
- The doctrine of man. His creation, essential nature, and fall.
- The doctrine of Christ. His essential nature, Incarnation, death and Resurrection.
- The doctrine of the Holy Spirit. His essential nature and work.
- The doctrine of salvation. Grace, regeneration, sanctification and glorification.

---

[26] https://reasonabletheology.org/cs-lewis-on-reading-old-books/

- The doctrine of the church. Its nature, its government, its sacraments, and its activity.
- The doctrine of the future. The return of Christ, the new heavens and earth.

Alongside that, it is always a good idea to get a good working knowledge of Israel and the church's history. There are many good books out there that will help you to formulate a thorough understanding of the history of the people of God and how God worked through that history.

My goal throughout the writing of this book has been to get you excited about this Bible that you hold in your hand. The health and future of local churches, and indeed the whole church is in the hands of those who read and know their Bibles; those who have learned in the quietness to discern the voice of God in the Scriptures, who understand theology and doctrine, and are able to communicate it clearly to the coming generation. May you be among them!

A Prayer Before You Start to Read the Bible

Dear Lord,

Please open my eyes so that I may see wonderful things in Your word, vistas of the kingdom that will draw my heart after You, truths that will set me free and cause my heart to run after You.

Please open my ears so that I may hear Your voice in the Scriptures, speaking words that are affirming, challenging, and even disturbing, words that will both build me up and never let me settle into complacency.

Please open my mind to understand the Scriptures, so that I may read them as You read them and see them in the light of heaven.

Please open my heart that I might receive Your words, so that my life may be the more conformed to Your image, that I might walk more fully in Your purposes and plans for me, and that I might partake and share even more in Your divine nature.

Amen.

Appendix of Recommended Books

Bibles

ESV Study Bible, (Crossway Bible, Illinois, 2007)
The NASB International Inductive Study Bible, (Precept Ministries, Oregon, 1993)

Concordance

NASB Exhaustive Concordance of the Bible with Hebrew, Aramaic and Greek Dictionaries. (Holman Bible Publishers, Nashville, 1981)

Hebrew and Greek words studies

Expository Dictionary of Bible Words by Lawrence O. Richards (Marshall Pickering, Basingstoke, 1988)
Vine's Expository Dictionary of Biblical Words edited by W.E. Vine, Merrill F. Unger and William White, Jn. (Thomas Nelson Publishers, New York, 1985)

Books

J.I. Packer, *Knowing God*, (Hodder & Stoughton, London, 1973)
Ralph Shallis, *From now on*, (STL Books, Kent, 1978)
T.C. Hammond, *In Understanding be Men*, (IVP, Leicester, 1977)
R.C. Sproul, *Knowing Scripture*, ((IVP, Illinois, 2016)
Gordon Fee and Douglas Stuart, *How to Read the Bible for all its Worth*, (Scripture Union, Bletchley, 1993)
Eugene Peterson, *Eat This Book*, (Hodder & Stoughton, London, 2006)
Michael Casey, *Sacred Reading – the Ancient Art of Lectio Divina,* (Ligouri/Triumph, Missouri, 1996)

Whole Bible Commentaries

New Bible Commentary: 21st Century Edition edited by D.A. Carson, R.T. France, Alec Moyer and Gordon J. Wrexham (IVP, London, 1994)

The IVP Bible Background Commentary: Old Testament edited by John H. Walton, Victor H. Matthews and Mark W. Chavalas (IVP, London, 2000)

The IVP Bible Background Commentary: New Testament by Craig S. Keener (IVP, London, 2014)

Bible Dictionaries

Zondervan Illustrated Bible Dictionary by Douglas and Tenney (Zondervan, Grand Rapids, 2011)

Systematic Theology

Kevin J. Connor, *The Foundations of Christian Doctrine*, (City Christian Publishing, 2005)

Kevin J. Connor, *The Foundations of Christian Doctrine Study Guide*, (Independently published, 2018)

Wayne Grudem, *Systematic Theology,* (IVP, Leicester, 1994)

Robert Culver, *Systematic Theology*, (Mentor, Ross-shire, 2005)

Background and historical

R.K. Harrison, *Old Testament Times*, (IVP, London, 1971)

F.F. Bruce, *Israel and the Nations*, (IVP, Leicester, 1998)

Merrill C. Tenney, *New Testament Survey*, (IVP, London, 1973)

Bibliography

Alexander, J. A. *Acts*. Edinburgh: Banner of Truth, 1980.
Armerding, Carl E. *Judges*. In *Zondervan Bible Commentary*. Grand Rapids, MI: Zondervan, 2008.
Atkinson, David. *The Message of Genesis 1-11*. Leicester: IVP, 1990.
Augustine of Hippo. *The Confessions of St. Augustine*. London: Andrew Melrose, 1905.
Baldwin, Joyce. *The Message of Genesis 12-50*. Leicester: IVP, 1986.
Balthasar, Hans Urs von. *Prayer*. London: Geoffrey Chapman, 1961.
Barclay, William. *The Gospel of Mark*. The Daily Study Bible. Edinburgh: St Andrew Press, 1975.
Barclay, William. *The Gospel of Matthew. Vol. 1*. The Daily Study Bible. Edinburgh: St Andrew Press, 1975.
Benedict of Nursia. *Saint Benedict's Rule*. Ampleforth: Ampleforth Abbey Press, 1997.
Binz, Stephen J. *Conversing with God in Scripture*. Frederick, MD: The Word Among Us Press, 2008.
Bonar, Andrew. *Robert Murray M'Cheyne*. Edinburgh: Banner of Truth, 1972.
Bosch, D. J. *Transforming Mission: Paradigm Shifts in Theology of Mission*. Maryknoll, NY: Orbis, 2008.
Bradfield, Bill. *On Reading the Bible*. Mineola, NY: Dover Publications Inc, 2005.
Bridges, Charles. *The Christian Ministry*. Edinburgh: Banner of Truth, 1976.
Bridges, Charles. *Psalm 119: An Exposition*. Edinburgh: Banner of Truth, 1977.
Bridges, Charles. *Proverbs*. Edinburgh: Banner of Truth, 1977.
Bright, John. *A History of Israel*. London: SCM Press, 1972.
Brown, John. *Hebrews*. Edinburgh: Banner of Truth, 1976.
Bruce, F. F. *Paul: Apostle of the Free Spirit*. Exeter: Paternoster Press, 1977.
Buchanan, Alex. *Bible Meditation*. Eastbourne: Kingsway Publications, 1987.
Bunyan, John. *The Holy War*. Edinburgh: T. Nelson & Sons, 1885.
Casey, Michael, OCSO. *Sacred Reading*. Liguori, MO: Liguori/Triumph, 1996.
Casey, Michael, OCSO. *Truthful Living*. Leominster: Gracewing, 2001.
Casey, Michael, OCSO. *Strangers to the City*. Brewster, MA: Paraclete Press, 2005.
Casey, Michael. *Toward God*. Liguori, MO: Triumph Books, 1996.
Cole, Alan. *Tyndale Commentary on Exodus*. London: Tyndale Press, 1973.
Culver, Robert. *Systematic Theology*. Ross-shire: Mentor, 2005.
Deane, Anthony C. *St. Paul and His Letters*. London: Hodder & Stoughton, 1942.
Dunn, James D. G. *The Theology of Paul the Apostle*. London: T&T Clark, 1998.
Eadie, John. *A Commentary on the Greek Text of the Epistle of Paul to the Ephesians*. New York: Robert Carter and Brothers, 1861.
Edersheim, Alfred. *Jesus the Messiah*. London: Longmans, Green and Co, 1916.
Erickson, Millard J. *Christian Theology*. 3rd ed. Grand Rapids, MI: Baker Academic, 2013.
Farrar, F. W. *The Life of Christ*. London: Cassell and Company Ltd, 1894.

Fee, Gordon. *The First Epistle to the Corinthians*. Grand Rapids, MI: Eerdmans, 1987.
Ferguson, Everett. *Backgrounds of Early Christianity*. Grand Rapids, MI: Eerdmans, 1987.
Ferguson, D. S. *Biblical Hermeneutics: An Introduction*. Atlanta: John Knox, 1986.
Foster, David. *Reading with God: Lectio Divina*. London: Continuum, 2005.
Foster, Richard. *Streams of Living Water*. New York: HarperCollins, 1998.
Furlong, Monica. *Merton: A Biography*. London: SPCK, 1995.
Gargano, Guido Innocenzo. *Holy Reading: An Introduction to Lectio Divina*. Norwich: Canterbury Press, 2007.
Garrett Jr., James Leo. *Systematic Theology. Vol. 1*. Texas: Bibal Press, 2007.
Graham, Billy. *Just As I Am*. Revised and Updated 10th Anniversary ed. New York: HarperOne, 2007.
Greenlee, J. H. *Introduction to New Testament Textual Criticism*. Revised ed. Grand Rapids, MI: Baker Academic, 1993.
Grubb, Norman. *C.T. Studd: Cricketer and Pioneer*. London: Lutterworth Press, 1939.
Grudem, Wayne. *Systematic Theology*. Leicester: IVP, 1994.
Guthrie, Donald. *The Pastoral Epistles*. London: Tyndale Press, 1973.
Hall, Thelma. *Too Deep for Words: Rediscovering Lectio Divina*. New York: Paulist Press, 1988.
Hammond, T. C. *In Understanding Be Men*. Leicester: IVP, 1977.
Harrison, R. K. *Old Testament Times*. London: IVP, 1970.
Henry, Matthew. *Commentary on the Whole Bible*. London: Marshall, Morgan & Scott, 1960.
James, Fleming. *Personalities of the Old Testament*. New York: Scribners, 1939.
John of the Cross. *Collected Works*. Washington, D.C.: ICS Publications, 1991.
Josephus, Flavius. *The Works of Flavius Josephus*. Translated by William Whiston. Edinburgh: Nimmo, Hay & Mitchell, 1895.
Judge, E. A. *Roman Empire*. In *New Bible Dictionary*, edited by J. D. Douglas et al., London: Inter-Varsity Press, 1970.
Kaiser Jr., Walter. *Exodus*. In *NIV Bible Commentary. Vol. 1*, edited by Kenneth L. Barker and John R. Kohlenberger III. London: Hodder & Stoughton, 1994.
Kempis, Thomas à. *The Imitation of Christ*. Peabody, MA: Hendrickson, 2004.
Kidder, Annemarie S. *The Power of Solitude*. New York: Crossroad Publishing Company, 2007.
Kidner, Derek. *Genesis*. London: Tyndale Press, 1973.
Kidner, Derek. *Ezra and Nehemiah*. Leicester: IVP, 1979.
Klein, William W., Craig L. Blomberg, and Robert L. Hubbard Jr. *Introduction to Biblical Interpretation*. Dallas: Word Publishing, 1993.
Leech, Kenneth. *Soul Friend: A Study of Spirituality*. London: Sheldon Press, 1980.
Leupold, H. C. *Exposition of Genesis. Vol. 1*. Grand Rapids, MI: Baker Book House, 1942.
Lewis, C. S. *The Magician's Nephew*. London: Grafton, 2002.
Lewis, C. S. *The Lion, the Witch and the Wardrobe*. London: Grafton, 2002.
Lewis, C. S. *The Magician's Nephew*. London: Grafton, 2002.

Lewis, C. S. *The Last Battle*. London: Grafton, 2002.
Lloyd-Jones, Martyn. *The Christian Soldier*. Edinburgh: Banner of Truth, 1977.
McAlpine, Campbell. *The Practice of Biblical Meditation*. London: Marshall, Morgan and Scott, 1981.
MacDonald, Gordon. *Ordering Your Private World*. Nashville: Thomas Nelson, 1985.
McDonald, H. D. *What the Bible Says About the Bible*. Eastbourne: Kingsway Publications, 1979.
McGrath, Alister. *Christian Theology: An Introduction*. 6th ed. Hoboken, NJ: Wiley-Blackwell, 2016.
Merton, Thomas. *On St. Bernard*. Kalamazoo, MI: Cistercian Publications, 1980.
Murray, Iain H. *D. Martyn Lloyd-Jones: The First Forty Years*. Edinburgh: Banner of Truth, 1982.
Nee, Watchman. *The Song of Songs*. Fort Washington, PA: Christian Literature Crusade, 1966.
Nee, Watchman. *Release of the Spirit*. Chichester: New Wine Press, 1965.
Nee, Watchman. *The Spiritual Man*. New York: Christian Fellowship Publishers, 1977.
Nee, Watchman. *The Ministry of God's Word*. New York: Christian Fellowship Publishers, 1971.
Nietzsche, Friedrich. *Human, All Too Human*. Ware: Wordsworth, 2008.
Okholm, Dennis. *Monk Habits for Everyday People*. Grand Rapids, MI: Brazos Press, 2007.
Packer, J. I. *God Has Spoken*. London: Hodder & Stoughton, 1979.
Packer, J. I. *Truth and Power: The Place of Scripture in the Christian Life*. Wheaton, IL: Harold Shaw Publishers, 1996.
Packer, J. I., and Parrett, Gary A. *Grounded in the Gospel*. Grand Rapids, MI: Baker Books, 2010.
Pierson, A. T. *George Müller of Bristol*. First published 1899. Pantianos Classics.
Peterson, Eugene. *Answering God*. San Francisco: Harper & Row, 1989.
Peterson, Eugene. *Eat This Book*. London: Hodder & Stoughton, 2006.
Peterson, Eugene. *Working the Angles*. Grand Rapids, MI: Eerdmans, 1987.
Peterson, Eugene. *Christ Plays in Ten Thousand Places*. London: Hodder & Stoughton, 2005.
Peterson, Eugene. *Practice Resurrection*. London: Hodder & Stoughton, 2010.
Peterson, Eugene. *Subversive Spirituality*. Grand Rapids, MI: Eerdmans, 1997.
Peterson, Eugene. *Leap Over a Wall*. San Francisco: HarperOne, 1997.
Peterson, Eugene. *The Jesus Way*. London: Hodder & Stoughton, 2007.
Peterson, Eugene. *A Long Obedience in the Same Direction*. Downers Grove, IL: IVP, 2000.
Peterson, Eugene. *The Contemplative Pastor*. Grand Rapids, MI: Eerdmans, 1989.
Pollock, John. *The Apostle*. London: Hodder & Stoughton, 1969.
Pollock, John. *The Master*. Wheaton, IL: Victor Books, 1984.
Ramm, Bernard. *Protestant Christian Evidences*. Chicago: Moody Press, 1953.

Sailhamer, J. H. *Genesis*. In *NIV Bible Commentary. Vol. 1*, edited by Kenneth L. Barker and John R. Kohlenberger III. London: Hodder & Stoughton, 1994.
Sanders, P. *Adrift: Postmodernism in the Church*. Nashville, TN: Gospel Advocate, 2000.
Sarah, Robert Cardinal. *The Power of Silence*. San Francisco: Ignatius Press, 2017.
Schreiner, Thomas. *Paul, Apostle of God's Glory in Christ*. Downers Grove, IL: IVP, 2001.
Scroggie, W. Graham. *The Unfolding Drama of Redemption*. Grand Rapids, MI: Kregel Publications, 1994.
Shallis, Ralph. *From Now On*. Bromley: STL Books, 1978.
Shannon, William. *Thomas Merton's Dark Path*. Toronto: Collins Publishers, 1987.
Smith, David. *The Days of His Flesh*. London: Hodder & Stoughton, 1910.
Sproul, R. C. *Knowing Scripture*. Downers Grove, IL: IVP, 2009.
Strong, A. H. *Systematic Theology*. London: Pickering & Inglis, 1970.
Tappy, Connie G. *Judges*. In *Eerdmans Companion to the Bible*, edited by Gordon D. Fee and Robert L. Hubbard Jr., Grand Rapids, MI: Eerdmans, 2011.
Tenney, Merrill C. *New Testament Survey*. London: IVP, 1973.
Tennyson-Arkels, Carolyn. *Under the Influence*. Bloomington, IN: WestBow Press, 2014.
Tillyer, Desmond. *Union with God: The Teaching of St John of the Cross*. London: Mowbray, 1984.
Torrey, R. A. *How to Study the Bible*. London: Oliphants Ltd, 1955.
Tozer, A. W. *The Pursuit of God*. Eastbourne: Kingsway Publications, 1982.
Tozer, A. W. *The Divine Conquest*. London: Oliphants, 1964.
Tozer, A. W. *Man the Dwelling Place of God*. CreateSpace Independent Publishing Platform, 2017.
Unger, Merrill. *Unger's Bible Dictionary*. Chicago: Moody Press, 1983.
Usher, R., and Edwards, R. *Postmodernism and Education: Different Voices, Different Worlds*. New York: Routledge, 1994.
Wesley, John. *The Works of Rev. John Wesley, A.M.* HardPress Publishing, 2019.
Wenham, David, and Walton, Steve. *Exploring the New Testament. Vol. 1*. London: SPCK, 2001.
Willard, Dallas. *The Spirit of the Disciplines*. San Francisco: Harper & Row, 1988.
Wright, G. E. *An Introduction to Biblical Archaeology*. London: Duckworth, 1960.
Wright, N. T. *Simply Jesus*. London: SPCK, 2011.
Wright, Tom. *How God Became King*. New York: SPCK, 2012.
Young, E. J. *Thy Word is Truth*. Edinburgh: Banner of Truth, 1972.

ARTICLES

Alexander, T. D. "Introduction to Genesis." In *ESV Study Bible*. Illinois: Crossway Bibles, 2008.
Birdsall, J. N. "Texts and Versions." In *New Bible Dictionary*, edited by J. D. Douglas. London: IVP, 1970.

Branch, Robin G. "How Was the Bible Passed Down to Us?" In *Eerdmans Companion to the Bible*, edited by Gordon D. Fee and Robert L. Hubbard. Michigan: Eerdmans, 2011.
Bruce, F. F., General Editor. "Acts." In *Zondervan Bible Commentary*. Michigan: Zondervan, 2008.
Gelston, A. "Sadducees." In *New Bible Dictionary*, edited by J. D. Douglas. London: IVP, 1970.
Hubbard, Robert L., and Gordon D. Fee. "What is the Bible?" In *Eerdmans Companion to the Bible*, edited by Gordon D. Fee and Robert L. Hubbard. Michigan: Eerdmans, 2011.
Judge, E. A. "Roman Empire." In *New Bible Dictionary*, edited by J. D. Douglas. London: Inter-Varsity Press, 1970.
Packer, J. I. "Infallibility and Inerrancy." In *New Dictionary of Theology*, edited by Sinclair B. Ferguson, David F. Wright, and J. I. Packer. Leicester: IVP, 1988.
Packer, J. I. "Inspiration." In *New Bible Dictionary*, edited by J. D. Douglas. London: Inter-Varsity Press, 1970.
Theonnes, Erik. "Biblical Doctrine." In *ESV Study Bible*, Illinois: Crossway Bibles, 2008.
Wessel, Walter W. "Mark." In *NIV Bible Commentary*, Vol. 2. London: Hodder & Stoughton, 1994.

E-SWORD

The International Standard Bible Encyclopaedia, article on *universal need of authority*
Andrew Robert Faussett, *Bible Dictionary*
Keil and Delitzsch, *Commentary on the Old Testament*
The International Standard Bible Encyclopaedia
William Hendrickson and Simon J. Kistemaker, *Baker's New Testament Commentary*
Thayer's Greek Definitions

ELECTRONIC SOURCES

http://www.guinnessworldrecords.com/world-records/best-selling-book-of-non-fiction/
https://www.biblesociety.org.uk/latest/news/bible-distributing-breaks-record-for-2014/
https://www.newstatesman.com/politics/religion/2020/04/how-coronavirus-leading-religious-revival
https://www.gospeloutreach.net/bible.html
http://plato.stanford.edu/entries/neitzsche/
https://www.crcna.org/welcome/beliefs/confessions/belgic-confession
https://www.icr.org/article/james-ussher-his-chronology-reasonable
http://www.RayStedman.org
http://bibleodyssey.org/people/main-articles/herod-the-great

About the Author

Alan Hoare has been exercising a pastoral and teaching ministry for nearly fifty years, whilst being married to his wife, Mo. Together they have five children (now mature adults) and eleven grandchildren.

Now fully retired from church leadership, he has turned his attention to writing, mentoring and occasionally preaching. His heart has consistently been to see Christians engage meaningfully with the Bible for themselves, putting down deep roots into a life-long relationship with the God the Father, Son and Holy Spirit.

Find out more at exploringscripture.co.uk

About Broad Place Publishing

Broad Place Publishing is a Christian imprint whose aim is to bring Jesus-centred books to the market. We want to see good-quality books, inspired by the Holy Spirit, brought to life and made available across the world.

We look to partner with authors and readers, developing new ways of working together, modelling Kingdom values. If you would like to support us, in prayer or financially, please go to broadplacepublishing.co.uk/support

For more information, go to broadplacepublishing.co.uk

Also from Broad Place Publishing

Books to encourage families in their walk with Jesus
by Joy Vee

The Kai Series (5-8s):
Kai: Born to be Super
Kai: Making it Count
Kai: Playing his Part

The Sienna Series (8-12s):
Love from Sienna
Left Out, Sienna?

The Petrov Series:
The Letters She Never Sent (8-12s)
They Whisper About Us (12+)

Adult Fiction

The Wanderer Series
by Natasha Woodcraft

"You shall be a fugitive and a wanderer on the earth."

1. The Wanderer Scorned
Cain & Abel reimagined

2. The Wanderer Reborn
Can hope triumph after the first murder?

broadplacepublishing.co.uk

www.ingramcontent.com/pod-product-compliance
Lightning Source LLC
Chambersburg PA
CBHW030255100526
44590CB00012B/410